Following Jesus to Burning Man

Recovering the Church's Vocation

Kerry D. McRoberts

Foreword by Leonard Sweet

Hamilton Books
A member of
The Rowman & Littlefield Publishing Group
Lanham • Boulder • New York • Toronto • Plymouth, UK

Copyright © 2011 by
Hamilton Books
4501 Forbes Boulevard
Suite 200
Lanham, Maryland 20706
Hamilton Books Acquisitions Department (301) 459-3366

Estover Road
Plymouth PL6 7PY
United Kingdom

All rights reserved
Printed in the United States of America
British Library Cataloging in Publication Information Available

Library of Congress Control Number: 2010937800
ISBN: 978-0-7618-5383-1 (paperback : alk. paper)
eISBN: 978-0-7618-5384-8

∞™ The paper used in this publication meets the minimum
requirements of American National Standard for Information
Sciences—Permanence of Paper for Printed Library Materials,
ANSI Z39.48—1992

For My Wife, Vicki—
#867—You Are My Inspiration
and
My Daughters
Kari & Traci—
Your Character Is Sacred in His Sight,
Your Children Will Call You
Blessed; Your Husbands Also, Praise You.

Contents

Foreword: Jesus Is Already There, at "Burning Man"	ix
Acknowledgments	xiii
Introduction: An E-P-I-C Recovery!	xv
The Church's Journey to Burning Man	xvi
1 Following Jesus to Burning Man	**1**
Following Jesus to Burning Man: "You Belong Here"	1
An EPIC Week in the Desert	3
The Week Begins	4
Watching for Cows and Cops	9
The Incarnation: Divinity Wrapped in Sinless "Burner"	9
2 "A Glutton and a Drunkard"	**11**
The Church's Vocation	11
Until You Become Like Us, You Do Not Belong Here	12
Christ's Table-Fellowship: This Man Eats with Sinners	13
Jesus' Table-Fellowship: Enacting Israel's Vocation:	
Mark 2:13–17 and Matthew 9:9–13: Jesus Attends a Party	14
Matthew 14:13–21, Mark 6:30–44, Luke 9:10–17,	
and John 6:1–13: A New Exodus	15
Mark 8:1–10 and Matthew 15:32–39: Inclusion in the	
Kingdom of God	16
Matthew 11:19 and Luke 7:34: "A Glutton and a Drunkard"	16
John 2:1–11: New Wine	17
Matthew 26:6–13, Mark 14:3–9, Luke 7:36–50,	
and John 12: 1–8: Offended Pious	18
Luke 11:37–54: External Purity/Internal Impurity	19

	Luke 14:1–24: One Greater than the Temple	19
	Luke 19:1–10: Exchanging Wealth for Poverty	21
	Matthew 26:17–30, Mark 14:12–26 and Luke 22:7–20: The Last Supper	22
	Luke 24:13–35: A Post-Resurrection Meal	23
	What Was Jesus for Israel?	24
	What Is the Church to Be for the World?	25
	Conclusion—The Church's Vocation: 'A Glutton and a Drunkard'	27
3	William Wilberforce and "Vital Christianity"	33
	Vital Christianity	33
	Christian Singularity	34
	Vital Christianity and Cultural Transformation	36
	Building Community	37
	Contextualizing the Gospel	38
	The Common Good	39
	Co-Belligerence	40
	Political Philosophy	41
4	Journeying to Burning Man: Recovering the Church's Vocation	45
	A Postmodern Community's Perspective	46
	Cultural Transformation in the Twenty-First Century	47
	Building Community	47
	Contextualizing the Gospel	48
	The Common Good	51
	Co-Belligerence	53
	Application: Kingdom Politics and Cultural Transformation	54
	A Politics of *Re-Form*	55
	A Politics of *Re-Connection*	56
	A Politics of *Re-Creation*	57
	Conclusion: Water Baptism and the Church's Vocation	58
5	'Jesus at the Java Stop': A Grassroots Application of Kingdom Politics	64
	Semiotics: Reading the Signs	65
	Common Good	66
	'Jesus at the Java Stop'	67
	A Grassroots Application of Kingdom Politics	68
	Doing Grassroots Cultural Transformation	69
	A Missional Journey: Phase 3: *Re-Create*: Minimum Time: An Organic Church is Always Adapting—Until the Return of Jesus Christ!	73
	Church Planting	75

Appendix 1 Discipleship: Interactive Everything!	77
Discipleship—Interactive Everything	78
Cultivate a Biblical World-View	78
World-Views and Semiotics	80
Practicing the Presence of Christ in the Market Place	80
Participation in Cultural Transformation	82
Participation in the Great Commission	83
Conclusion: 21st Century Discipleship Is Interactive Everything	83
Appendix 2 Web Sites	85
Bibliography	87

Foreword:
Jesus Is Already There, at "Burning Man"

I come out of the holiness tradition. Sometimes we were called "holy rollers," but mother taught us to say the following to people who mocked us as holler rollers: "I'd rather roll into heaven than dance into hell." In the Pilgrim Holiness church, instead of giving a ring to your fiancee, you gave a watch. "She got her watch" is how you referred to an engaged woman. When a girl showed up in church with a watch, everyone started talking. I once asked mother: "But the watch is more gold and a bigger circle." Mother smiled as she replied, as if her next words settled everything: "But it's 6 inches higher, and not around the finger."

As a product of the holiness tradition, I had the privilege of experiencing first-hand the two Protestant pilgrimages. The first is the family reunion, especially in its southern form. The second is the journey to a sacred space, most often an ancestral church, cemetery, or meeting ground. For me the two came together in one: a Pilgrim Holiness camp-meeting outside of Albany called "Victory Grove Camp" and a Free Methodist camp-meeting outside of Saratoga Springs called "Pine Grove Camp." Both the family reunion and the sacred grounds were found for the Sweet family in the yearly summer pilgrimages to these two camp-meetings.

Camp meetings arose among the plain-folk on the southwestern frontier, but they soon spread everywhere. First called "brush arbor revivals," "tent meetings," "protracted meetings" or "open air cathedrals," by the early days of the 19th century, one name stuck: "camp-meetings." From the very beginning camp-meetings exhibited pronounced emotionalism and bizarre behavior. This is partly because camp-meetings were forms of male evangelism, out-of-doors settings where men could let their emotions out without fear of being ridiculed or seen as unmanly. And when emotions long pent up are permitted out, one can never predict or control what comes next.

Virginia Baptists held camp meetings as early as 1767, but camp meetings were not brought to the evangelical world's attention until 1799 on a Kentucky frontier. There, legendary meetings at Red River in 1799, Gaspar River in 1800, and most famously Cane Ridge in 1801, under Methodist, Presbyterian and Baptist auspices, brought camp meetings to the forefront of America's religious consciousness, where they would remain as evangelical expressions of popular religious piety until the mid-40s. Unprecedented crowds of ten to twenty-five thousand were matched by spectacular conversions of notorious drunkards, criminals, prostitutes, and disbelievers, not to mention the emotional spectacles of the "exercises" (falling, drinking, barking, dancing, laughing, etc.) and "impressions" (marriage, business, health, etc.)

Such goings-on scared away many evangelicals. By 1805 the Baptists and Presbyterians drew back from sponsoring camp meetings, leaving them to the Methodists both to defend, as Lorenzo Dow (who introduced camp meetings into England in 1807) did so systematically in his *History of Cosmopolite*, and to develop, as they did with such great success, with six hundred camp meetings held in 1816, and one thousand in 1820. The first Methodist bishop, Francis Asbury, demonstrated his enthusiasm for camp meetings when he chronicled the numbers saved and sanctified in an 1806 camp meeting in a letter to one of his presiding elders. Asbury concluded with the remark 'Oh, my brother, when all our quarterly meetings become camp meetings, and one thousand souls shall be converted, our American millennium will begin" (7 November 1806, 357, in *Journal* III [1958 ed.]. Not until Methodists demonstrated that emotions could be wiped cleaner from religious expressions at camp meetings did other evangelical denominations begin to participate in them again.

Camp meetings were a favorite target for popular literature, especially novels, where sarcasm and criticism of camp meetings often came to a head. There was not a dearth of material for critics to work with. Apart from what contemporaries called the "religious catalepsy," there was the phenomenon of mixed motives with which people came to camp meetings. Some women came for the dress parade and cooking showdowns; some wealthy came to pawn their power; some politicians came to seek votes; some merchants came to hawk wares; some town rowdies came to stir up trouble; some whiskey peddlers came with more than cider in their canteens; and some young people came for reasons which are best not to scrutinize too closely. In 1807 on the Wyoming-New York circuit, a not uncommon camp-meeting brawl occurred after local ruffians had integrated the women's side of the camp meetings tent and the men went to their aid. The result was a free-for-all and numerous arrests, including a presiding elder who struck someone with a hard right and landed in jail for assault. The presiding elder was joined a little later by a red-faced Methodist bishop, who had been arrested for fighting. A famous passage in Mark Twain's *The Adventures of Huckleberry Finn* (1885) satirized the ignorant, indecorous, gullible features of those who attended an Arkansas camp meeting in the 1830s. Catherine Reed Williams' *Fall River* (1933) allegedly documented the gross immorality promoted by camp meetings, and a popular anthology of poems with the lead one entitled *The Camp Meeting* (1819) was sexually explicit in describing how such events led to more souls being made than saved.

Perhaps camp meetings fell under the greatest suspicion among evangelicals, however, for their mixing of business with pleasure. In the words of a character in a Mary Clemmer Ames' *Eirene* (1871), "The whole scene bore witness to what it was–a great religious picnic, in which material pleasure and human happiness blended very largely with spiritual experience" (68).

A frontier camp meeting was a profoundly sensuous experience, which was a source both of its power (for its defenders) and its peril (for its detractors). At camp meetings evangelicals enjoyed God, battled Satan, and consecrated the commonplace. They sensed the presence of God in smell: in the fragrance of nature's incense–the clean scent of the sawdust trail, the sweet odor of sap form the pine trees, the breath of smoke from the fire altars. They sensed the presence of God in sight: a theologically-based architecture determined the layout of tents in the elliptical design of the camp. Camp meetings were first called "open forest cathedrals" because they were held in nature's temple under the canopy of clouds by day and the chandelier of stars by night, when the night torches would cast their eerie shadows across the congregation in tents. They sensed the presence of God in touch: through the feeling of the earth for a mattress and splintery logs for a pew; through the touching of each other in forgiving embrace at the mourner's bench, in the kiss of peace at the 'glory pen,' and in the hand clasping ceremony at the speaker's platform. They sensed the presence of God in sound: with the voice of singing, praying, and preaching. Evangelicals loved to pine after upcoming camp meetings for they knew that 'great shouters" would be there, as well as "plain preachers" who pioneered in the use of anecdotes and illustrations. The poetry of camp meetings' spiritual ballads, praise hymns, and revival spirituals was not among the finest of American literature, but its emotionalized theology was straight from the heart of experience, and bold in expressing the free, joy and forgiveness evangelicals found in the Christina life. There are some reports that preaching got so intense at camp meetings that people forgot to eat, but more often it was the case that God was sensed through taste; people looked forward to camp meetings for a month as a yearly oasis of hospitality in a desert of frontier loneliness and isolation —hospitality shown through sumptuous meals and cookouts. One report suggests that the August

1801 Cane Ridge camp meeting dispersed finally only because the 20,000 to 30,000 attenders ran out of food.

If all this is starting to sound vaguely familiar, it's because it is. "Burning Man" is a new 21st century pilgrimage site, a Google world equivalent of the camp-meetings that inaugurated the 19th century. Kerry McRoberts' book, "Following Jesus to Burning Man: Recovering the Church's Vocation," is a marvelous introduction to this pilgrimage ritual by people who are fundamentally on a spiritual quest. There are 2000 camp meetings still being held every year across the world. Burning Man is a pagan type camp-meeting full of signs that point to our culture's spiritual exile.

But what participants in Burning Man don't know, and what the church has yet to learn, is that Jesus is already there at "Burning Man." Hence the significance of Mac's title: "Following Jesus to Burning Man." Long before we ever arrive anywhere, Jesus is already there and up to something. Just as the "gospel" was first proclaimed in Galilee, the place of Gentiles, the light is meant to shine in darkness. Read this book and find out how.

Leonard Sweet
George Fox Evangelical Seminary
Portland, Oregon
June 24, 2010

Acknowledgments

For over 30 years my tribe has been the Assemblies of God and in my context, Dr. George Wood, Charles Crabtree, John Bueno, Dale Carpenter, Dan Womack, David Grant, Lew Shelton and Ray Jennings all exemplify, in a most extraordinary manner, what it is to truly be a "minister of the Gospel."

Among my friends are men of rare character: Don Conant, Chuck Vanasse, Mike Fogaras, Tom Nishimura, Brian Kelly, Dave Jones, Charles Worthington, Scott Womack, Marv Osburn, Ken Smalley, Steve Roderick, Jonathan Palmer and Nick Fossen.

My advisors and cohort, George Fox Evangelical Seminary, Len Sweet, Kent Yinger, and Chuck Coward, Lars Rood, Henry Berg, Fourie van den Berg, Bryan Benjamin, Randy Groves, John Frank, Quintin "Q" Moore, Brian Ross, Jake Youmans, Jeff Tacklin, Chris Roush, Denis Bell and Greg Glantz will always be close to my heart.

My former congregations: Bethel Assembly of God, Pe Ell, Washington; Sumner Assembly of God, Sumner, Washington; and Kings Circle, Corvallis, Oregon, have been instruments of e-p-i-c spiritual experiences that "color" the pages of this book.

Northwest University, Trinity Bible College, North Central University (Glen Menzies, Phil Mayo, Tracy Paino and Gordon Anderson are extraordinary men of God), and the Assemblies of God Theological Seminary, have been my teaching contexts.

Finally, Vicki, my wife of 38 years, Jim and Kari, Jamie and Daphne Schultz; Matt and Traci, Ryan, Hayley and Payton Brakefield complete my life.

Introduction: An E-P-I-C Recovery!

Postmodernism, according to Leonard Sweet, is E-P-I-C:[1]

- Postmodernists passionately seek Experiences: "When postmoderns say 'Get real;' they don't mean 'Prove it!' and they don't mean 'Give me the Truth.' They mean 'Give me an experience, and then I'll see whether or not I believe it.' For something to be real, it doesn't need to be proven—only experienced."
- Postmoderns are driven to Participate, they're not spectators: "Postmodern culture is an 'age of participation,' an 'age of access.'"
- Postmoderns don't respond to logical propositions; they are responsive to a seemingly infinite array of Images, signs, and symbols: "Postmodern is another name for interactive everything."
- And Postmoderns love Community: "The declining quality of human relationships makes people yearn for community all the more"—postmodernism is E-P-I-C.[2]

Recalling Jonah's disobedience to God's calling, just over twenty years ago I wrote: "The church's flight to its own Tarshish, confusing godly separation with isolationism, is resulting in the turning over of our culture to the ungodly by default."[3]

This book is devoted to our culture's recovery and transformation by means of the church's Spirit-empowered application of Kingdom Politics. More explicitly, this book is an exhortation for the Evangelical Church in North America to be E-P-I-C[4]:

1. By discovering and **E**xperiencing the presence of Jesus Christ in every corner of the postmodern culture; and **P**articipating in *missional* ministry with him, *wherever* he is present;
2. By reading the cultural **I**mages, signs and symbols and effectively contextualizing (incarnating) the gospel, especially in the culture's most hurting places;
3. By practicing the politics of *Re-Form, Re-Connection* and *Re-Creation* a Spirit empowered, covenant **C**ommunity is capable of effectively recovering and transforming our culture.

This book is not intended to *teach* church leadership how to do cultural transformation (a "one-size fits all" approach is characteristic of modernity) rather it is intended to *facilitate* church leadership in their journey to discover for themselves effective means of transforming their particular cultural context.

THE CHURCH'S JOURNEY TO BURNING MAN

Chapter 1: "FOLLOWING JESUS TO BURNING MAN" is an epic account of the author's "X-treme" experience in the Nevada desert. "Following Jesus to Burning Man" is a metaphor for the church's vocation—the church is to be for the world, what it cannot be for itself.[5]

Chapter 2: "A GLUTTON AND A DRUNKARD," redefines the church's vocation in the context of a biblical world-view in contrast to the external radical dualism characteristic of the Evangelical Church on a large scale today. Jesus' table-fellowship gives symbolic redefinition to the church's vocation; the reformed church is to be for the world what it cannot be for itself.[6]

Chapter 3: "CHRISTIAN PRAXIS IN HISTORIC PERSPECTIVE: WILLIAM WILBERFORCE'S 'VITAL CHRISTIANITY,'" introduces the great reformer and political statesman William Wilberforce (1759–1833) and the Clapham Group. This chapter is an historical example of how the church's vocational redefinition in England transformed British culture.

Chapter 4: JOURNEYING TO BURNING MAN: CUTURAL TRANSFORMATION: A transformed church is able to transform culture! What would cultural transformation look like in 21st century America?

Chapter 5: "JESUS AT THE JAVA STOP": THE APPLICATION OF KINGDOM POLITICS," confronts the challenge of the postmodern world through reading the signs, and seeing the world differently. The proposal of a narrative apologetic and the grassroots application of Kingdom Politics—*a politics of re-form; a politics of re-connect* and *a politics of re-create* are discussed in chapter 5.

Appendix 1: DISCIPLESHIP—INTER-ACTIVE EVERYTHING! Discipleship in Postmodern America is "Interactive Everything!" Church leadership needs to create interactive environments for Christians to participate in the facilitation of their own discipleship.

Appendix 2: RECOMMENDED WEB SITES, is a listing of web sites featuring missional ministries, churches and cultural research resources.

NOTES

1. Leonard Sweet, *Soul Tsunami* (Grand Rapids, MI: Zondervan, 1999), 215–220.

2. The essential nature of humanity is understood in terms of relationships; the individual stands under "erasure."

3. Kerry D. McRoberts, *New Age or Old Lie?* (Peabody, MA: Hendrickson Publishers, 1989), 127.

4. My use of the term, "Evangelical Church" relates to churches that primarily believe: God's Word is revelatory, authoritative and literal unless the context requires a metaphorical understanding; salvation is experienced through rebirth; and the church is called to "witness" locally and globally. Therefore, the term "Evangelical" includes Pentecostals and Fundamentalists.

5. I am indebted to N.T. Wright for shaping my thinking about the Church's vocation. See, for example: *Response,* Seattle Pacific University, "A Conversation With N. T. Wright," Summer 2002, Volume 28, Number 2 (http://www.spu.edu/depts/uc/response/summer2k5/features/conversation.asp Downloaded: 08/15/2005).

6. Re: footnote #5, this slogan is a specific example of my application of N.T. Wright's theme for the church's vocation: "Before you can say, 'as Jesus to Israel, so the church to the world,' you have to say '*because* Jesus to Israel, *therefore* the church to the world'"—*The Challenge of Jesus, Rediscovering Who Jesus Was and Is* (Downers Grove, IL: Inter-Varsity Press, 1999), 183.

Chapter One

Following Jesus to Burning Man

As Highway 447 spiraled downward towards the desert basin of Black Rock City, I caught up with a very strange spectacle: a debauched and lewd looking caravan decorated with phallic symbols that seemed to stare at me as I passed. This was my first glimpse of the Burning Man crowd. Plunging myself into a celebration of human exploitation, depravity, and idolatry with 30,000 pagans in the relentless heat of the Nevada desert was suddenly very unsettling! And the notion that this would be Jesus' kind of crowd was far removed from my imagination.

The Incarnation plunges God in Christ into the guts of human life; Jesus exchanged the throne of heaven's glory for the margins of his creation. This book uses "following Jesus to Burning Man" as a metaphor for the church to recover her vocation and be for the world what it cannot be for itself. This chapter introduces the Burning Man metaphor through the author's "X-TREME" experience in the Nevada desert.

FOLLOWING JESUS TO BURNING MAN: "YOU BELONG HERE"

Burning Man is a sensuous "Corinthian-like" pagan festival annually taking place in the remoteness of Nevada, on the desolate moonscape of an ancient lake bed, the last week of August and the first few days of September. Black Rock City is re-birthed each year when the Burning Man community comes together. Black Rock City has the appearance of what you might imagine the aftermath of nuclear radiation fallout looks like. It's ominous, deathly; nothing is growing there, nothing is on the horizon but the intense glare of the sun. The staging of Burning Man is haunted by images of the apocalypse: camouflaged army half-tracks, tanks and jeeps mounted with machine guns, bazookas and other army surplus.

I arrived at Black Rock City in the early Monday morning hours. Cars were backed up from the entry point to Burning Man for at least two miles; the gridlock resembled Friday afternoon on the Santa Monica Freeway. As the cars slowly moved forward, I could see taillights dispersing in all directions beyond the entry point to Burning Man; more than an hour passed before I finally entered through the gates and into Burning Man's mysterious netherworld.

Before I could proceed further, a young woman ran up to the side of my Honda Pilot yelling, "Welcome home! Welcome home!" Her torso was covered with long black fur, she had a fur bear-like head covering with ears on the top, long sheer black sleeves covered her arms, and black-knit nylons covered her long, skinny legs.

"Hey, thanks," I said. (I'm sure the look on my face was similar to Charleston Heston's shocked look after he glimpsed the chimp on the pony following his re-entry into the atmosphere of the "planet of the apes.")

"Are you a virgin?" she asked.

"Ah, yeah, this is my first time here." I perceived her implication but I had to make sure!

"Get out of your car, run up to that girl with the long black hair and long brown fur coat (she was also wearing white "go-go" boots) and tell her you're a virgin," the young woman said.

I obediently got out of my Honda Pilot and walked briskly up to the young woman. The Burning Man website says, "You belong here...."[1] I wasn't sure about that. The website also says, "You're not the weirdest kid in the classroom." Yeah, I was pretty sure all of these people were the weirdest kids in the classroom!

"Hi, this is my first time at Burning Man," I said. The young woman grabbed my hand tightly, threw back her head, looked towards the full moon, and let out a spine-tingling howl. I anxiously invoked a prayer: "Lord, you didn't get out of the car at the Nevada border when I stopped for gas did you? Where are you?" She dragged me over to a line of guys who were taking turns striking a large bell with a steel rod; she held my hand tight until it was my turn. When I stepped up to the bell, I took the steel rod and struck it with a Mantle-like swing! "He's in, he's in," the people yelled. "Welcome to Burning Man!" I was hugged and mobbed; it was like my walk-off homer had just put Block Rock City, Nevada in the playoffs!

After entering through the gate, a billow of alkaline dust enveloped me. I came out on the other side driving across the playa.[2] A ranger drove up beside me and asked, "What the *#@! are you doing?"

"You got me!" I said. "Give me a hint."

The ranger and I connected, and he shared his story. An adjunct professor at the University of California, Santa Barbara, he was widowed a few years ago; he brings some of his wife's ashes to Burning Man every year to spread a portion of them ceremoniously on the ground at the "temple" on Sunday mornings. Impassioned about his pagan spirituality, he said, "Paganism allows me to honor all gods." After showing me where to find a camping spot, he kindly warned me, "You'll see a lot of nudity, so be prepared." I drove all the way to the end of a road the ranger directed me to and took a left; I found an open space on the margins of Black Rock City to camp.

It was about 4:00 a.m. and I was exhausted. I fell asleep in the back of my Honda Pilot as I sifted through my conversation with the pagan ranger. Purely subjective claims about God or gods reduce to meaningless tautologies; if no particular religion or spirituality is right or wrong, the notion, "Paganism allows me to honor all gods," is meaningless.

AN EPIC WEEK IN THE DESERT

Burning Man is E-P-I-C: everyone **E**xperiences, everyone **P**articipates in the mystique of Burning Man; Burning Man's eclectic array of **I**mages of hope, fear and the future are reflected in new "realities;" and new worlds emerge from a primal drive in Burners to survive together in **C**ommunity.

The Burning Man activities catalogue, *Who, Where, When*, contains sixty pages of epic pagan events, displays, and lectures for Burners' individual and group participation:

Bare your hopes and fears at the Black Rock Super-therapist. Need more? Enjoy a Martini at the Barry White Memorial Bar while soaking in our hot tub." A sampling of other Burner experiences include participation in sado-masochistic bondage at the "Temple of Atonement"—a "professionally staffed sanctuary and dungeon, a place of respect, vulnerability, and beauty," offering "an exquisite trip into the world of pleasure and pain." The "Burning Desires Meeting," offers recovery for burned-out Burners. Other activities include, "Yoga in the Morning," "Guerrilla Poetry Open Mic . . . bringing peace rhymes for wartimes and words of hope for a better future," "Gnome Adoption Agency: Come adopt your very own garden gnome," "Vodka Snorting," "Divination Station," "Brutal Rationality Counseling: 'You've tried therapists, drugs, perhaps even a few retreats, but you know you're still not right in the head . . . We are not board certified anything,'" "Princess Reform School," "AA Meeting— Queers, Crackpots and Fallen Women," "Think Different, Think Evil, Wanted: Intelligent, motivated, resourceful, easily corrupted, and ethically shortsighted individuals to participate in an exciting global domination initiative," "Burning Man: The Musical!, Greasier than Grease, cattier than Cats and hairier than

Hair!," "Erotic Tickling Workshop," "Nature's Magical Mystery Tour," "The God Box Afternoon Opening: An equal opportunity mystical experience, open to all Burners," "Naked Gun: Cool off during the hottest part of the day!," "One Stop Service Station: Do you fear the past and hope for the future? Have your cards read by Lisa with a spanking to grow on," "God/Goddess Encounter: Come and be initiated into the art of experiencing your lover as a god or goddess," "Messiah for A Minute: Might you be the Messiah? We will decide and reward you accordingly . . . Accept our devotion or feel our wrath," "Porn Stars on the Esplanade! The naughtiest game on the playa;" "Arabian Nights Couples Party: Bisexual couples welcome in our darkened den of hedonism," "The XEssential Experience . . . a live performance that connects light and sound to exemplify the creative potential of the conscious human spirit," "Porta-Pottie Party," "Blood of Mary Communion," "Black Rock Bible Burning Party: This is a baptism by fire into the rational future. Join us as we bid farewell to the irrational religions of the past and clear the way for the New Scientism. Bring your Bibles, Torahs, Qurans, Rig Vedas, Dianetics, Bhagavad Gitas, Tao Te Chings, etc., and ritualistically set them ablaze. We will burn them all," and "Occult Cocktail & Mummy Wrapping: Magicians, Sorcerers, Witches, Sacred Whores, Chaotes, Priests and all other practitioners of Thee Magickal Arts take heed . . . We will be unwrapping a freshly unearthed Mummy to observe first-hand the ancient Mysteries of the mighty Egyptians, as well as exchanging knowledge and techniques to hone our mastery of the Unseen Forces."

The ultimate finale of the Burning Man experience is the turning of "The Man" in the playa's center into a flaming inferno at the end of the week. This is conceived as a transcendent experience celebrated in a plurality of ways: the postmodern participant views the erasure of the all-powerful "I;" Buddhists celebrate the cycle of death and rebirth on the wheel of life; Hindus see the absolution of the personal into the impersonal universal soul, and to the mystic, heaven and earth melt into one in the ignited frame of the Man.

THE WEEK BEGINS

The water truck sprays down the cracked, dusty, alkaline paths throughout Black Rock City every morning. It also provides a morning shower for a half-dozen to a dozen naked screaming men (and some days, a woman or two) running behind it.

As I walked to the porta-potties, I observed that tutus, long skirts in a variety of bright colors, tight satin panties (pink appeared to be in vogue), tight tank tops with spaghetti straps and exposed midriffs, tight fitting, brightly colored mini-skirts complimented with a tee-shirt sporting a vulgar image or saying or both appeared to be the chosen male fashion for the day. The women were less into fashion; the preferred style for many appeared to be high-cut black tennis shoes, shorts, or Catholic school-girl type plaid skirts (they went beyond bare midriffs). For others, men and women, full-nudity seemed to ease the anxiety over what to wear for the day's activities.

I spent my first day walking around the camp area on the esplanade and the playa, taking pictures of the strange art, talking to people, and hearing their stories. Sychar and his wife are from New York City. Sychar owns a studio; he is an artist, a photographer, and a documentary film maker; he has been dreaming about the day he could come to Burning Man.

"Mick," (his real name is Ebal; he does a great Mick Jagger imitation) is originally from Afghanistan and is now an American citizen (his earliest childhood memories of America are Richard Nixon's resignation from his presidency and the New York Knicks winning the NBA championship.) Ebal is with another man, Ryan. Ebal and Ryan are stewards for a major airliner. Katie came to my campsite to borrow some tools so she could put a basket on her bicycle. Katie is with several of her friends; they are all students at the University of Oregon. At sunset, the young coeds ritualistically run around topless in the open-space beyond the last row of campsites. Russell is a middle-aged man from Santa Cruz, California. Russell's camp is set up behind mine in an area off-limits to any cars.

People stayed up all night and all day, they never seemed to sleep, though I am sure many of them caught up on their rest while passed out during the day. Large, float-like monstrosities, lit up with various colored tube lighting and blaring music, went up and down the dusty alkaline paths running through the campsites throughout the night; alcohol, drugs and riotous hedonistic pleasure fueled Burners' desires.

While at my campsite, I sat on a chair next to my Honda Pilot and watched, listened to, and greeted people. Many people stopped and talked to me. Sychar and his wife were very open to the gospel. We talked about spirituality and Sychar's perceptions of the church. Burners are hungry for spiritual experience, but the last place on earth they can imagine finding it is in the church! Russell and I started a conversation about the interconnectedness of the essential elements (particles) of the universe that would continue through the week. Katie and her friends were very intrigued with my descriptions of the "sins of my youth" at the University of Oregon, and my Christian testimony and how I became a pastor.

A sudden, raging windstorm shattered the tranquility of the third evening; fierce winds swept across the desert floor. My tent collapsed immediately; I placed my cooler, my camp stove and anything else I could find that would not blow away on top of my tent to keep it from being airmailed back to Oregon! I ran over to Russell's campsite to help him tie down his awning. Jack, a young man from Eugene, Oregon, outfitted in shorts, boots, and an old, World War I "Mad Max" type leather flight cap (the ears were flapping wildly in the wind), and black round goggles quickly showed up to help.

While we struggled to secure Russell's big awning into the desert floor, Jack looked up at me and yelled, "Do you have hope, Mac?" I looked at Jack, he was covered with the desert's alkali and orange dirt; he looked like a big goggled chicken breast rolled in flour and corn meal! "I sure do Jack," I said. "My hope is in a person, my hope is in Jesus Christ; he's the Source of my faith, he's my hope!"

"Wow!" Jack resounded. "Are you like some big time Christian, Mac?"

Jack is desperately searching for any hope he can find for the future of the planet; he fears some great catastrophic event such as a comet colliding with the earth, a nuclear war, or worldwide pestilence may destroy the cosmos. With camping gear, tarps and tents flying by us and as Russell's awning was consuming the wind like a huge parachute, dragging us across the desert floor, I offered Jack a better story in place of his dreadful tale of faithlessness, fear and future destruction; faith, hope and love can be known in Jesus Christ; Jesus brings hope and assurance, the future is in his hand.

We finally got Russell's camp firmly anchored. Jack left to help another Burner in distress and Russell invited me to stay and talk with him. Russell ascribes to Buddhist ethics and relates them to quantum physics.[3] I listened to him intently; Russell is a brilliant but refreshingly humble man. Russell's world-view perceives the universe as an interconnected, organic whole.

"But without a transcendent," I asked. "How can ethics be possible? How can the physicist, himself a part of everything interconnected in the universe, speak of justice without a transcendent?"

Russell readily conceded the physicist is part of the interconnectedness of all things but he countered by asserting that, "the need of a transcendent does not necessarily point to the God of the Bible."

"The most profound thing about the God of the Bible is that not all things are the same to him," I retorted. "He possesses personality; He has moral character. Some things in His creation conform to His character, other things do not. This sharply distinguishes the God of biblical Revelation from the concept of God in Hinduism or Buddhism, in these religions, ultimate reality is an impersonal universal identified in essence with the cosmos; pantheism fails to distinguish between good and bad, righteousness and evil, compassion and exploitation; human rights are meaningless."[4] Russell and I decided to take up our conversation later, and I departed for another long walk.

Following my walk around the playa, talking to people about their art, and listening to their stories, Ryan came across the path to talk to me. "Why are you here?" he asked.

"I want to be more like Jesus, Ryan," I said.

Ryan, while still standing, turned towards the tents, travel trailers, canopies and motor homes that are Black Rock City, temporary home to thirty thousand Burners, and remarked, "Yeah, Jesus spent a lot of time with tax collectors, prostitutes and sinners; just like all of us."

My eyes filled with tears, "Yeah, Ryan, just like all of us."

Later, Ebal (Mick) came back across the dusty path, bringing his chair with him, he sat down, and asked, "So why are you here?"

"Because I want to be more like Jesus," I said. "Why are you here, Mick? Why did you come to Burning Man?"

Mick said he was seeking a "transcendent experience." There are as many interpretations of the meaning of a "transcendent experience" as there are people who come to Burning Man; nevertheless, most agree a hoped for, deeply felt spiritual experience draws people to the Nevada desert.

Ebal was raised Muslim, his parents are devout Muslims, but Ebal no longer practices Islam and is rather inclined towards Buddhist ethics without a comprehensive embrace of Buddhism. Ebal attended a Catholic School in Brooklyn as a child and is familiar with basic Christian teachings. His response to why I came to Burning Man was theologically Islamic: "Jesus was a great prophet in line with the other prophets."

"Tell me, Mick," I asked, "When Jesus came into Jerusalem, the final week of his life and the common people praised him as the 'Blessed One' and he went into the Temple and turned over the tables of the money changers and ran them out of God's house, what do you think was going on?"

"He was acting like a prophet," Ebal said.

"Yes, Mick, his actions were prophetic. Like Jeremiah, he prophesied the near future destruction of the Temple as climatic to his ministry, and the Temple was destroyed by the Romans in A.D. 70. But his actions in the Temple indicated he was much more than a prophet. His disruption of the daily sacrifice, more specifically, his interruption of the preparation of the paschal lambs to be sacrificed and eaten by faithful Jews for Passover at the end of the week, was because he himself was to be sacrificed at the end of the week; he is God's Paschal Lamb 'who takes away the sins of the world.'

The Temple cult ritual was means for the forgiveness of the sins of the people; Jesus was replacing the Temple and the Passover lamb with himself and his work on the Cross as means of atoning for the people's sins—Jesus did and said things reserved only for Yahweh to do and to say.[5]

Either Jesus was the divine Son of God, come down from heaven, and therefore he was much more than a prophet, or he was a false prophet. And if Jesus was a false prophet, the prophetic lineage in Islam breaks down; Muhammad is not a prophet. But if Jesus possesses divine authority to do and say things reserved only for Yahweh, if he shares the throne of Yahweh, then Muhammad and all of humanity must bow their knee to him and worship him as Lord."

Ebal was silent for a few minutes. I reached over to him and placed my hand on his shoulder, "Have I offended you, Mick?" "No," he said. "I'll be back." Mick picked up his chair and walked back across the path.

I took another long walk. People were lined up outside the "Erogenous Zone" on the playa's boardwalk, the esplanade. Next door, women were learning how to slide up and down a pole; I quickly discerned this had nothing to do with a Black Rock City volunteer fire department! A vampire, four long fangs protruding out of his mouth, his shoulders draped in a red cape, walked by; I got a great picture! (The vampire was far less frightening than the naked elderly couple following closely behind him!)

On my way back to my campsite, I encountered two men, both were at least six-feet-six; their naked bodies were totally coated with white alkaline! They were apparently depicting they were survivors from the raging wind storm the night before!

The porta-potties were getting really full; it was a matter of survival until the end of the week. As I arrived back at my car, Sychar and his wife stood in front of their van facing my campsite. A friendly young couple, they were really enjoying their experience at Burning Man. They touched my heart, and I hoped somehow I could show them Jesus and his love for them.

Ebal (Mick) and Ryan came back across the path to continue our conversation. Mick resounded, "God is glorious; God is above all creation; God is incomprehensible; God doesn't have a son; God doesn't have relatives; God stands alone as holy and unapproachable; God would never reduce himself to becoming man, that's blasphemy! The Jews believe in only one God, like Islam; God is one!"

"Do you know, Mick," I asked, "The Jews considered the Messiah to be the Son of David?"

"Yes," he responded. "And David was Jewish, was he not?"

Mick again responded, "Yes."

"Then how is it David said, 'The Lord said unto my Lord, sit at my right hand until I make your enemies a footstool for your feet;' if David calls the Messiah 'Lord,' how can he then be his son?"

Ebal was unresponsive so I continued. "In the Sermon on the Mount, Jesus boldly challenged Israel's controlling narrative, the story by which they live: 'You have heard that it was said . . . But I tell you.'[6] 'You have heard it was said, Do not commit adultery. But I tell you that anyone who looks at a woman lustfully has already committed adultery with her in his heart.' 'You have heard that it was said, Love your neighbor and hate your enemy. But I tell you: Love your enemies and pray for those who persecute you.' Jesus is replacing the Torah, the source of Israel's controlling narrative, with himself; he is not nullifying the Torah, he is its fulfillment. Jesus consistently said and did things reserved only for Yahweh to say and to do."

Mick was contemplative and Ryan excused himself to go back across the path to prepare dinner. I again reached over to Mick and placed my hand on his shoulder, "Mick, I agree with you, God would not reduce himself to become a man; God added man to himself, this is the whole point of the gospel, God added man to himself and plunged into the depravity, the wickedness, the evil, the sin and the suffering of our world for our sakes. 'For you know the grace of our Lord Jesus Christ, that though he was rich yet for your sakes he became poor, so that you through his poverty might become rich,' wrote Paul. You've come here for a transcendent experience; God can give you that and so much more, he can give you a relationship with himself through faith in his Son Jesus Christ. What do you think Mick?"

Before Mick departed for dinner, he kindly told me how impressed he was that someone like me would be so open to others, especially the type that would attend Burning Man. Mick and I stood to our feet and hugged one another. Mick's sentiments moved me deeply; there are no "others" just "one another," we all have a story and we all need Jesus.

WATCHING FOR COWS AND COPS

The end of the week had arrived. Before leaving Burning Man, I went back over to Russell's campsite to say goodbye. Russell holds a PhD in physics from MIT; this confirmed my suspicion that I was not his intellectual equal.

I went next door to Sychar's and his wife's campsite. Sychar and his wife were preparing to leave, but Sychar took a moment to tell me he could not help overhearing my conversations with Mick and various people who stopped by my campsite. He said he listened intently; he had never heard the gospel expressed as he had heard it at Burning Man. He reached out to me and hugged me, holding me in his arms for a minute. Sychar and his wife wanted to know about churches in New York City they could check out and hear things like they did at Burning Man!

As I was leaving Black Rock City in my rearview mirror, I stopped at the gate. An old gray bearded, rotund man stumbled out of a little green shack; he was busy pulling up his pants as he came up to the side of my car, "Did you have a good time?"

"Yeah," I said, "I had a great week with my best Friend, Jesus of Nazareth!"

"Ummm . . . Well, make sure you look out for cows and cops! They're watching for us." I assumed he meant the cops, not the cows, were watching for all of us "Burners."

THE INCARNATION: DIVINITY WRAPPED IN SINLESS "BURNER"

Dallas Willard gives us a glimpse of the humility and poverty of the Incarnation: "When Jesus deals with moral evil and goodness, he does not begin by theorizing. He plunges immediately (Matthew 5:21–44) into the guts of human existence; raging anger, contempt, hatred, obsessive lust, divorce, verbal manipulation, revenge, slapping, suing, cursing, coercing, and begging."[7] Jesus had not abandoned me at the Nevada border when I stopped for gas, he had gone on ahead of me where he was waiting for me to join him in his work on the extreme cultural margins—wherever Jesus is, nightclubs, Burning Man or Sunday morning service, the kingdom of God is present. Although many of the people Jesus loves to hang out with make me uncomfortable, I want to be where Jesus is and do what he is doing! Chapter 2 is revelation of where Jesus is and what he is doing.

NOTES

1. http://www.burningman.com, copyright 1989–2005 black rock city, llc.

2. The playa is the center and main surface where "The Man" is erected among a variety of art displays. Over 100 structures, sculptures, and constructs litter the playa.

3. Buddhist ethics refer to the Four Noble Truths and the Eightfold Path. The first noble truth acknowledges the existence of suffering; the second noble truth acknowledges that the cause of suffering is the craving desire for sensual pleasure; the third noble truth is the ending of suffering and the fourth leads to the eightfold path: the first step is right views, accepting the four noble truths and the eightfold path; right resolve, the renouncing of sensual pleasure is the second step; right speech, do not lie, slander, etc., is the third step; right behavior, do not destroy any living creature, is the fourth step; right occupation, earn your livelihood is the fifth step; right effort, preventing evil and promoting good is the sixth step; right contemplation, free of desire and sorrow is the seventh step and the eighth step is right meditation, entering the four degrees of meditation. See, for example, Josh McDowell and Don Stewart, *Handbook of Today's Religions* (San Bernardino, CA: Here's Life, 1983), 304–324.

4. This argument is a paraphrase of an argument delivered by Francis Schaeffer, "Christian Faith and Human Rights," quoted in John Warwick Montgomery, *Human Rights and Human Dignity* (Grand Rapids, MI: Zondervan, 1986), 113.

5. N.T. Wright is the author of this slogan I am paraphrasing here. See, for example, Wright, *The Challenge of Jesus, Rediscovering Who Jesus Was and Is* (Downers Grove, IL: Inter-Varsity Press, 1999), especially chapter 5, "Jesus & God," pages 96–125.

6. Matthew 5:21–48 records six antitheses, subversive to Israel's controlling narrative, that include: murder, adultery, divorce, oaths, justice, and love for one's enemies.

7. Dallas Willard, *The Divine Conspiracy* (San Francisco: Harper, 1997), 129.

Chapter Two

"A Glutton and a Drunkard"

Contemporary culture has fallen down a rabbit's hole into a world of discontinuous change—"curiouser and curiouser."[1] A paradigmatic shift of seismic proportions from modernity to post-modernity is taking place. Most adult Christians heard the gospel and learned to "flesh it out" in a modernist context. In this context, life is progressing forward, success is just around the corner, and every problem eventually works itself out. However, modernity's shelf-life is expiring; the closing of the twentieth century was marked by a rapidly eroding trust in modernism and its vision of human reason as a universally valid foundation for knowledge.

The church is now confronted with new ways to think about her faith and how it relates to the world. Many Christians, however, do not see the church making a difference in the culture in which they spend their forty to sixty hour work weeks.

Unfulfilled prophecies of revival and renewal have left many Christians disillusioned. Church has become boring; it is the last place people think of when they are searching for creative ways to make a difference in society. And although we live in a day where people are willing to go way out of their way to find spiritual power, even to the remoteness of the Nevada desert, they would never think of looking for it in the church!

THE CHURCH'S VOCATION

The church's vocation is to be for the world what Jesus was for Israel.[2] In this chapter, we will develop what Jesus was for Israel, and what the church is to be for the world; a survey of Jesus' table-fellowship in the Gospels will serve as a model. But before we proceed with the aforementioned theme of this chapter, we will address the sectarian mindset of much of the church—the mindset of much of the contemporary church restricts God's people from joining Jesus on the margins. Finally, we will close this chapter by developing a narrative from our survey of Jesus' table-fellowship for the purpose of constructing a symbolic paradigm of what Jesus was for Israel and what the church is to be for the world.

UNTIL YOU BECOME LIKE US, YOU DO NOT BELONG HERE

Significant portions of the evangelical church see themselves at the center as powerful, successful, and established. The church's perception of herself at the center entices her into believing that anyone who is not with her is either against her or worse, they are simply irrelevant. Jim Wallis describes church life and theological perceptions "at the center" from "left" to "right":

> God is *personal, but never private.* If God is not personal, there is little meaning to faith. It merely becomes a philosophy or a set of teachings from religious figures who died long ago. Without a personal God, there is no personal dimension to belief. There is no relationship to God, no redemption, salvation, grace or forgiveness. There is no spiritual transformation without a personal God, and no power that can really change our lives beyond mere self-improvement. In today's world, there is one over-riding and key distinction in all of the religion that is growing—a God who desires relationship with each person. Much of liberal religion has lost the experience of a personal God, and that is the primary reason why liberal Christianity is not growing. And without a personal God, liberal faith will never grow.[3]

Progressive (Liberal) Christianity's impersonal, unknown god is a mere impulse incapable of defining evil, much less imposing moral imperatives; Liberal Christianity is powerless and lifeless.

> However, that personal God is never private. Restricting God to private space was the great heresy of twentieth-century American evangelicalism. Denying the public God is a denial of biblical faith itself, a rejection of the prophets, the apostles, and Jesus himself. Exclusively private faith degenerates into a narrow religion, excessively preoccupied with individual and sexual morality while almost oblivious to the biblical demands for public justice. In the end, private faith becomes a merely cultural religion providing the assurance of righteousness for people *just like us.*[4]

An external radical dualism (as opposed to an internal dualism wherein the heart is properly set apart unto God in Christ) is symptomatic of "restricting

God to private space."⁵ A radical dualism creates a mental "gulf between the shadowy and impure world of matter, time and body and the changeless world of beauty, truth, and goodness known to the spirit and the intellect rather than the senses."⁶ The "changeless world of beauty, truth, and goodness" is *privatized* in the church: creation is fallen and corrupt and therefore culture is essentially evil and beyond redemption. Consequently, the church is seized by an excessive preoccupation "with individual and sexual morality while almost oblivious to the biblical demands for public justice."

The church's mental apartheid seduces her into posturing herself at the center; she is wealthy and powerful and the exclusive presence of the kingdom of God. The church's pathology constructs walls instead of bridges and expresses to the culture: "Come to us and become 'just like us' and then we will love you."

An external radical dualism is a systemic problem in large portions of the evangelical-fundamentalist church. An external radical dualism keeps the church from connecting her internal faith to the world around her and consequently, it subverts her obedience to her vocation to be for the world what it cannot be for itself.

CHRIST'S TABLE-FELLOWSHIP: THIS MAN EATS WITH SINNERS

"This man welcomes sinners and eats with them" (Luke 15:2). Jesus' open table-fellowship with sinners was controversial and symbolic; however, rather than illuminating, Israel's controlling narrative concealed the symbolic significance of Jesus' table-fellowship.⁷ For the marginalized, the "sinners" who gathered around Jesus to hear him (Luke 15:1) the symbolic meaning of their relationship with Christ was clear: relationship with Jesus assured a place setting at the messianic banquet.

Excluding the three meals surveyed below in the homes of Pharisees, there are eight meals that explicitly reveal the kingdom of God, and all of these meals place Christ on the cultural margins with first century Burners—"sinners, tax collectors and prostitutes." Christ's table-fellowship is, therefore, revelation of where the church will find Jesus. Jesus plunges into the guts of human existence; he is on the margins among the poor, exploited, and disenfranchised.

Jesus' welcome of the poor and the outcasts was a sign that the real return from exile, the forgiveness of sins, and the renewal of the covenant was taking place: "The 'resurrection' was coming into being; and if the new age was dawning, those who wanted to belong to it would (as in Deuteronomy and Jeremiah) have to repent."⁸

The motif of Christ's table-fellowship manifesting the kingdom of God is uniquely dispersed throughout the gospel accounts of Jesus' table-fellowship:

> Of all the means by which Jesus could have chosen to be remembered, he chose to be remembered by a meal. What he considered memorable and characteristic of his ministry was his table-fellowship. The meal, one of humankind's most basic and common practices, was transformed by Jesus into an occasion of divine encounter. It was in the sharing of food and drink that he invited his companions to share in the grace of God. The quintessence of Jesus' redemptive mission was revealed in his eating with sinners, repentant and unrepentant alike.[9]

The unifying themes of Christ's table-fellowship are: (1) an inaugural eschatology: Jesus was announcing the coming of the kingdom of God; (2) a restoration eschatology: Jesus was enacting Israel's return from exile, the forgiveness of their sins and the renewal of Yahweh's covenant; and (3) a realized eschatology: the kingdom of God about to burst into human history through Jesus is the first-fruits of a still future kingdom to come.

We properly (Biblically) infer from the unifying themes of Jesus' meals (particularly the eight meals with his disciples and the marginalized) that they are divinely intended to foreshadow the wedding feast of the Lamb at the close of the age.[10]

Jesus' enactment of the coming kingdom of God and the future messianic banquet was viewed as scandalous because he extended Yahweh's covenant to all the wrong people.[11] Nevertheless, Jesus consistently appears to believe that his presence constitutes the kingdom of God. This is an outstanding theme of the first of the eleven meals surveyed in this chapter.

JESUS' TABLE-FELLOWSHIP: ENACTING ISRAEL'S VOCATION: MARK 2:13–17 AND MATTHEW 9:9–13: JESUS ATTENDS A PARTY

Perhaps Jesus appeared to some to be more of a party animal than a Messiah on such occasions as his appearance at Matthew's house where a crowd of "sinners and tax collectors" just like Levi, himself a former despised toll-collector, were present for a festive party.[12]

Mark states that at this early period in Jesus' ministry, "there were many who followed him" (Mark 2:15). By way of his eating with the ceremonially unclean and the morally wicked, Jesus subverts social conventions, but what appears scandalous in the eyes of the Pharisees is in reality the manifestation of the kingdom of God.[13]

Ben Witherington observes that Jesus' calling of Levi and his companions (Mark 2:14) points to messianic forgiveness. Consequently, the meal Jesus shared with Matthew and his friends symbolized the anticipated messianic banquet at the end of the age.[14]

Moreover, Blomberg acknowledges the "imperfect tense for 'they were following' could suggest ongoing action and some measure of commitment to Jesus over a period of time."[15] Mark's implication is clear: these tax collectors and sinners have already repented.[16]

Messianic images from Isaiah (25:6–9) reveal Christ's holy presence having invaded the formerly unholy company of Levi and his friends. The kingdom of God belongs to the poor in spirit who have recognized Christ's kingship in his impoverished state; Levi and his friends are celebrating Jesus' acceptance of themselves and their consequent entry into the kingdom of God.[17]

MATTHEW 14:13–21, MARK 6:30–44, LUKE 9:10–17, AND JOHN 6:1–13: A NEW EXODUS

The second meal surveyed is revelation of a new Exodus. The new Exodus Jesus is enacting does not distinguish between the ceremonially clean and the unclean of Israel. All four gospels record Jesus' feast with 5,000 people. Only Mark alludes to the gathered crowds as "sheep without a shepherd" (Mark 6:34).[18] Mark's allusion appears to point to messianic significance. Mark's narrative repeatedly places Jesus in solitary, remote places (Mark 6:32; 35). Mark draws his readers into a story of Jesus' reenactment of the Exodus; the multiplication of bread in the wilderness is a sign of covenant renewal.[19]

The feeding of the multitude in the wilderness appears to point to the promise of the Messiah's feasting with men in the wilderness (Isa. 25:6–9); however, the austerity of the feeding is more reminiscent of the Exodus.[20] The imagery of a new Moses miraculously multiplying the fare of a common meal to a spiritually wandering people anticipates a restored, renewed Israel (Mark 6:41). The majority of people present are common Galileans including farmers, fishermen, and homemakers.

Blomberg observes, "By Pharisaic standards, one must describe this gathering as ritually impure."[21] The remote location does not allow for cleansing rites to be observed much less for it to be by invitation only; the unclean and the ritually clean sat side-by-side rejoicing together in their inclusion in the kingdom of God.[22] Jesus' symbolic redefinition of the kingdom of God is grassroots and God's apocalyptic drama is enacted on the margins. Consequently, Christ's table fellowship is marked by inclusion; albeit relationship with Jesus and entrance into the Kingdom is preceded by repentance (Mark 1:15).

MARK 8:1–10 AND MATTHEW 15:32–39: INCLUSION IN THE KINGDOM OF GOD

The third meal surveyed is revelation of the new Covenant. The new Covenant does not distinguish between Jew and Gentile. Mark and Matthew's accounts are parallel revelations of another miraculous feeding of a multitude. A large crowd of 4,000 people have been listening to Jesus for three days, and during this time, they have had nothing to eat (Mark 8:2).

Jesus is concerned for the peoples' physical welfare; they need food before their departure for some have come from a long distance (Mark 8:3). Witherington comments about those who have traveled a long distance to see and hear Jesus:

> Very clearly the first feeding indicates Jesus manifesting himself to Israel as the new Moses or David. . . . It is true that both stories take place in an isolated or deserted location, an allusion perhaps to manna in the wilderness, but as Hurtado points out, at v.3 it is stressed that some have come from far off, a phrase often used to speak of Gentile foreigners from distant lands (Isa. 60:4; Jer. 46:27; and material found only in the Greek version of Jer. 26:27 and 38:10). The emphasis in Mark 8 is quite clearly on Jesus feeding Gentiles, though of course the audience is mixed since it also involves some of the disciples.[23]

Whereas imagery of Moses, the Exodus and God's feeding of the Jews in the wilderness with the manna from heaven again surfaces, Mark's focus appears to be on Jesus' extension of the thrust of the renewed covenant to the Gentile world. Jews and Gentiles together are no longer in exile, the forgiveness of sins and inclusion in the kingdom of God is not by means of the Temple cult ritual or ethnic identity but through relationship with God's Messiah, Jesus.

The eschatological banquet is clearly in view in Mark's account of Christ's miraculous feeding of another great crowd in the remote wilderness. Jesus' promise that "many will come from the east and the west, and will take their places at the feast with Abraham, Isaac and Jacob in the kingdom of heaven" (Matt. 8:11) must certainly point to Gentiles.

MATTHEW 11:19 AND LUKE 7:34: "A GLUTTON AND A DRUNKARD"

Jesus' unqualified acceptance of society's riff-raff was revelation of the coming of the kingdom of God; however, Jesus' critics, the religious establishment, were provoked by appearances of inappropriate behavior for a prophet of the kingdom. In the broader context, John the Baptist is pictured living an ascetic lifestyle; he calls penitent Israel out to the wilderness to be baptized in preparation for the coming kingdom of God.

Contrarily, Jesus announces the coming kingdom of God through his joyous enactment of the eschatological banquet with his friends, the tax collectors and sinners. Although their message is the same, neither prophet of the coming kingdom is able to please "this generation."[24] Consequently, John is accused of having "a demon" and Jesus is accused of being a "glutton and a drunkard" (Matt. 11:16–19).[25]

Jesus describes John as the last of the Old Testament prophets and "the Elijah who was to come . . . He who has ears, let him hear" (Matt. 11:13–15),[26] but the marginalized Son of Man is a stumbling block to those abhorred by his scandalous table fellowship.[27] Christ's friends, however, the tax collectors and sinners, view his eating with them as a tangible symbol of their salvation and their "meals together were an expression of their new relationship with Jesus, which was celebrated as though it was a new relationship with God."[28]

Jesus offered forgiveness of sins on his own authority, replacing the Temple and Torah with trust in himself, and he included all the wrong people in the coming kingdom of God. Jesus, therefore, confronts his accusers with the truth that, "the tax collectors and the prostitutes are entering the kingdom of God ahead of you" (Matt. 21:31). Christ's table fellowship reveals the spiritual character of the kingdom of God; Jesus' enactment of the eschatological banquet embodies Israel's hope of return from exile, the forgiveness of her sins and the restoration of the covenant.[29]

JOHN 2:1–11: NEW WINE

John's account of the miracle of changing water into wine at the wedding in Cana recalls Jesus' parable of children in the marketplace (Matt. 11:16–17). Unlike the children who refused to dance to the music of the flute, Jesus appears to be enjoying the wedding festivities, which include the consumption of wine.

When the wine runs out, Jesus' mother informs him of the need of more wine. Jesus directs the servants to fill six stone water jars (John 2:3; 6–7). Each of the jars holds between twenty and thirty gallons of water. Jesus instructs the servants to take a cup of the water to the wedding-master for him to taste it. When the man in charge of the wedding banquet drinks from the cup, he is amazed at the quality of the wine because customarily, the best wine was served first and the cheaper wine later. The water Jesus turned into wine is of the highest quality!

The water transformed by Jesus into approximately 120–180 gallons of wine was poured out of jars used for Jewish purification; this sign points to the transformation of the old wineskins into new wineskins for the new wine of the coming kingdom of God (Mark 2:22).

MATTHEW 26:6–13, MARK 14:3–9, LUKE 7:36–50, AND JOHN 12:1–8: OFFENDED PIOUS

The Pharisees see themselves at the center; they define themselves by who they exclude. Since Jesus spends much of his time with all the wrong people, the pious despise him. The three meals that follow in this survey, therefore, lack the joy and celebration of the first five and the last three meals.

Jesus ate with a variety of people, usually in an atmosphere of celebration, though not always. The people Jesus normally kept company with were considered to be beyond the bounds of respectable society. Again, this was perceived as improper behavior for a prophet of the kingdom.[30]

The setting for this meal is not the margins but the home of a Pharisee, Simon. Rather than celebrating with Jesus, Simon was deeply offended by what he viewed as a seemingly intimate exchange in his home between a woman "who had lived a sinful life in the town" and Christ (Luke 7:37). Simon is immediately critical of Jesus. This ritually impure woman touches Jesus; surely if this man is a prophet, thought the Pharisee, Jesus would be aware of this woman's spiritual condition.[31] Luke 7:38 describes the woman's actions: while weeping at the feet of her Lord, the woman's tears began to cover Jesus' feet. The woman began wiping Jesus' feet with her long hair. She then poured costly perfume from an alabaster jar on Christ's feet. Blomberg describes the passion exhibited in the woman's actions:

> Luke's use of the verb form stresses the repeated, ongoing nature of each stage of the woman's actions. She was standing 'weeping' (*klaiousa:* an ongoing present-tense participle); she 'began to wet his feet' (indicating that she continued to do so); and she was kissing him (the imperfect *katephilet,* indicating ongoing past action). The anointing is likewise described in the imperfect tense (*eleiphen*).[32]

Simon's offense escalates and Jesus confronts the Pharisee's displeasure with a parable: "Two men owed money to a certain moneylender," says Christ. "One owed him five hundred denarii, and the other fifty. Neither of them had the money to pay him back, so he canceled the debts of both. Now which of them will love him more?" (Luke 7:41–42). Simon acknowledges the obvious, the man with more debt would be the most grateful (Luke 7:43).

In Luke 7:44–46, Jesus informs Simon that the humble gestures of the woman such as the washing of his feet, the welcoming kiss, and the anointing on his head, though not required, displayed a heart full of love because her many sins have been forgiven (the woman's actions indicate she had a prior relationship with Jesus). Jesus says to the woman, "Your sins are forgiven" (Luke 7:48). The offense of the pious Pharisee is now almost without bounds because Jesus announces that he himself is making the Temple cult ritual obsolete; Christ is inaugurating the kingdom of God but the self-righteous are unable to see God's gift of salvation in Jesus.

LUKE 11:37–54: EXTERNAL PURITY/ INTERNAL IMPURITY

This meal's setting is the home of a certain Pharisee and, once again, the occasion is not marked by celebration but rather a series of sustained judgment-warnings against the Pharisees because of their hypocrisy.[33] Rather than preparing for the meal through ceremonial cleansing, Jesus promptly enters the Pharisee's home and seats himself (Luke 11: 37–38). The host Pharisee is shocked but appears to say nothing.[34]

Whether Jesus has discerned the heart of the Pharisee or perhaps simply witnessed an expression of astonishment on his face, Christ initiates an assault on the external display of piety by the Pharisees, which is disconnected from any internal faith, humility, and charity (Luke 11:39–41).[35]

Luke refers to Jesus as "the Lord" (Luke 11:39) placing Jesus over all of the guests assembled, to include the host. Christ alone, not the "foolish people" reclining at the table with him, possesses the unchallenged authority to judge between deviant and righteous behavior (Luke 11:40ff). Jesus' inauguration of the kingdom of God and his restoration eschatology is too large for many among the Pharisees to see; they are too focused on ritual purity and the common man's admiration of themselves to see the significance of Christ's solidarity with the poor and the outcasts (Luke 11:42–54).

LUKE 14:1–24: ONE GREATER THAN THE TEMPLE

An outstanding theme of the last of the meals in the home of a Pharisee reveals the clash between Jesus' restoration eschatology and the political agenda of Israel's religious leaders. Jesus is again hosted by a "prominent Pharisee" in his home "one Sabbath" (Luke 14:1). Blomberg observes that when the gospel writers mention the Sabbath in connection with Jesus' activities they are usually setting the stage for conflict with the Pharisees and their legal tradition.[36]

A man suffering from dropsy sits in front of Jesus (Luke 14:2). While the Pharisees rivet their attention on Jesus and his every move, Christ abruptly confronts his accusers: "Is it lawful to heal on the Sabbath or not?" (Luke 14:3). While his accusers sit in silence, Jesus takes the man by the hand and heals him in direct violation of the Pharisaic interpretation of work on the Sabbath (Luke 14:2–6).[37] This appears to be a trap for not only was Jesus "being carefully watched" (Luke 14:1) to see if he would take the bait and heal on the Sabbath, the Pharisees had conspired together following Jesus' last meal in a Pharisee's home, "to catch him in something" (Luke 11:54).

Luke's transition has Jesus asking his accusers if they would rescue their son or an ox on the Sabbath, (Luke 14:4–5). Again, the Pharisees refuse to acknowledge Christ.

Following his observance of the guests carefully choosing the places of honor to sit for this meal, Jesus tells a parable pointing to the potential humiliation some may suffer when asked to give up their seat of honor for a less honorable seat (Luke 14:7–11).

In verses 16–24, Jesus tells a second parable of those who were invited to a "great banquet" but sent back excuses for why they could not attend (Luke 14:16–20). When the servant delivering the invitations reported all the excuses given to him to his master, the "owner of the house" became angry and remarkably ordered his servant to invite those generally considered ceremonially unclean in the eyes of the Pharisees (Luke 14:21–23). And those originally invited to the banquet will be turned away forever (Luke 14:24).

As the narrator, Luke forms another transition between the two parables; after hearing the first parable, one of the guests at the table remarks to Jesus, "Blessed is the man who will eat at the feast in the kingdom of God" (Luke 14:15). This comment, focusing as it does on the eschatological banquet, appears to strike at the heart of the controversy between Christ and the Pharisees.[38] Wright proposes:

> The clash between Jesus and his Jewish contemporaries, especially the Pharisees, must be seen in terms of *alternative political agendas* generated by *alternative eschatological beliefs and expectations*. Jesus was announcing the kingdom in a way which did not reinforce, but rather called into question, the agenda of revolutionary zeal which dominated the horizon of, especially, the dominant group within Pharisaism. It is not to be wondered at, therefore, that he called into question the great emphases on those symbols which had become the focal point of that zeal: Sabbath, food taboos, ethnic identity, ancestral land, and ultimately the Temple itself.[39]

Jesus affirmed Israel's destiny and vocation but to do this, he had to subvert the Pharisaic interpretation of Israel's story, particularly how the Second Temple Jewish controlling narrative was expressed in the nationalistic symbols. The Second Temple Jewish controlling narrative did not include people outside the Jewish community. The Targum to Isaiah 25:6 envisages Yahweh preparing a meal for all nations but instead of honor, inescapable plagues overcome the Gentile world. Contrary to this mindset, Jesus must restore the original meaning and thrust of the Abrahamic Covenant.[40]

Through his calling people to repentance, forgiving their sins and welcoming them into the kingdom of God, Jesus was proclaiming that in himself, "something greater than the Temple is here. . . . [But] wrapped in her own aspirations," Israel could not "recognize the coming of the kingdom when it stood before her in flesh and blood."[41]

The following sections address those who welcome the coming kingdom. The significance of Christ's solidarity with the poor and the outcasts reaches the heart of a man formerly indifferent to their plight.

LUKE 19:1–10: EXCHANGING WEALTH FOR POVERTY

Zacchaeus is a "chief tax collector" and, therefore, a very wealthy man at Israel's expense. Consequently, Zacchaeus was despised by the Pharisees and the Jewish people in general who regarded him as the moral equivalent of a leper (Luke 19:2), but Zacchaeus desperately "wanted to see who Jesus was" (Luke 19:3).[42]

Zacchaeus is, however, too short to see over the large crowd gathered for Jesus' arrival in Jericho, so he climbed a sycamore tree that was directly in Jesus' path. Jesus looked up, saw Zacchaeus perched in the tree, and said, "Zacchaeus, come down immediately. I must stay at your home today" (Luke 19:5). To the shock of the crowd, who would have been inclined to view Jesus' willingness to stay with Zacchaeus as tantamount to sharing in his sin, Zacchaeus scurries down the tree and gladly welcomes Jesus into his house (Luke 19:6–7).[43]

Zacchaeus publicly announces his repentance and his corresponding intention to follow Jesus (Luke 19:8). I. Howard Marshall comments on the remarkable character of Zacchaeus' testimony:

> The statement of Zacchaeus is to be understood as a reaction to the initiative of Jesus and to the objections of the crowd. In order that Jesus may be freed from the suspicion of consorting with a sinner he makes a public declaration of his intention to live a new life. In such a situation a declaration of intent was an adequate sign of repentance. At the same time, his action is to be seen as an expression of gratitude to Jesus for his gracious attitude to him, and as an example of the sort of change in life that should follow upon the reception of salvation.[44]

Zacchaeus' repentance did not require him to go to the Temple and offer a sacrifice; what was traditionally obtained through the Temple and the sacrificial system, Jesus provided for Zacchaeus in Jericho at the foot of a sycamore tree. Wright observes, "This was the real scandal. He behaved as if he thought (a) that the return from exile was already happening, (b) that it consisted precisely of himself and his mission, and hence (c) that he had the right to pronounce on who belonged to the restored Israel."[45]

MATTHEW 26:17–30, MARK 14:12–26 AND LUKE 22:7–20: THE LAST SUPPER

Jesus' last meal with his disciples before his crucifixion reveals his belief that the Kingdom is arriving in his person and work and consequently, Israel is being restored under the renewed reign of Yahweh. The synoptic Tradition asserts that the last meal Jesus shared with his disciples before his death was the Passover meal (Matt. 26:17, Mark 14:12, Luke 22:7).[46] Jesus and his disciples gather in the evening, in Jerusalem, for the meal (Matt. 26:20). The meal appropriately ends with a hymn, probably one of the *Hallel* Psalms (Matt. 26:30, Mark 14:26).[47]

The head of the household traditionally explains the different parts of the Passover meal in relation to the Exodus narrative. A Jewish person hears a story of return from exile, the forgiveness of sins, and the renewal of the covenant spoken of by the ancient prophets. The Exodus is Israel's story. Israel's controlling narrative was ongoing; year after year, the story pointed to Israel's God and his return to once again reign as the sovereign King. This particular meal was the occasion for Jesus to point to a new Exodus that was taking place in and through himself; Yahweh's kingdom-purposes are being fulfilled in Christ.

Jesus places the meal in an eschatological context. He takes the bread, gives thanks, and breaks it. He then passes portions of the bread to each of his disciples saying, "Take and eat; this is my body" (Matt. 26:26). Wright suggests, "According to the *Mishnah*, the unleavened bread of Passover was explained by Gamaliel (a contemporary of Jesus) as signifying the redemption from Egypt."[48] Jesus clearly identifies himself as Israel's means of redemption.

In a similar manner, Jesus takes the cup, offers it to his disciples and says, "Drink from it, all of you. This is my blood of the covenant, which is poured out for many for the forgiveness of sins," (Matt. 26:27–28). Jesus' words, "This is my blood of the covenant" recalls Moses' act of sprinkling the blood from the sacrifice on the people at Sinai and then announcing to them: "This is the blood of the covenant that the Lord has made with you" (Exod. 24:8).

The synoptic Tradition stresses Jesus' blood "is poured out for many" (Luke has "poured out for you," 22:20). Matthew and Mark's versions are linked to Isaiah 53, and Matthew adds Jesus' shed blood is "for the forgiveness of sins" (Matt. 26:28). Jesus' last meal with his disciples points to the inauguration of the Kingdom (Matt. 26:29, Mark 14:25/Luke 22:16). Israel is no longer in exile; the nation's sins are forgiven and the covenant is renewed through Yahweh's representative, Jesus the Messiah.

The Last Supper, Christ's final Passover meal with his disciples, has meaning only within an apocalyptic, eschatological context; a new age is dawning, new creation is beginning and not only Israel, but "all nations will blessed" through the new Exodus and the manifestation of the kingdom of God in and through Jesus of Nazareth.[49]

LUKE 24:13–35: A POST-RESURRECTION MEAL

Through the Resurrection, God reclaims His creation and makes all things new. The last meal surveyed is revelation of the beginning of new creation. Luke's narrative of the Easter Sunday journey of two of Jesus' disciples and a "stranger" from Jerusalem to Emmaus invokes images of the messianic banquet. Wright offers insight into the disciple's sharing of a meal with the "stranger" in their home at the end of the seven-mile journey (Luke 24:28–32):

> I wish to make one point about the way in which Luke has told the story. It concerns the central symbol, carefully repeated that lies at the heart of the Emmaus narrative. *Jesus is recognized when he takes the bread, blesses it, and breaks it* (24:30). The heart is warmed, says Luke, when scripture is expounded so as to bring out the true story, and the Lord is known in the breaking of the bread. The two belong together, interpreting each other and together pointing to the new world, the new vocation, the kingdom of God, and above all to Jesus himself as the climax of Israel's history and now Lord of the world.[50]

Jesus' "breaking of the bread," as a central feature of Luke's Easter narrative (and the common theme of Jesus' table fellowship throughout the gospels), envisages the kingdom of God and anticipates the coming eschatological banquet.[51]

Luke's narrative of the resurrected Jesus is cast in the context of the grand narrative of Second Temple Jewish hope of restoration and renewal. Judaism's controlling narrative conceived of resurrection as Yahweh's vindication of Israel and the inauguration of the kingdom of God. Hence, at the break of day, while the light was still struggling with the darkness that first Easter morning, no conscientious Jew living under the inflexible rule of Rome would have conceived of such wild notions of Israel's exilic restoration; the forgiveness of her sins and the renewal of the covenant with God.[52]

As the risen Christ catches up with the two grieving disciples on their journey home from Jerusalem, he abruptly intrudes into their conversation asking them what they are talking about (Luke 24:17). Their response is laced with hopelessness and despair: "Jesus of Nazareth . . . He was a prophet, powerful in word and deed . . . They crucified him . . . We had hoped that he was the one who was going to redeem Israel" (Luke 24:19–21).

The disciples' inability to recognize Jesus is understandable in light of Jewish eschatological expectations and the Resurrection. The "idea that 'the resurrection' has split into two, with Jesus' resurrection coming forwards into the middle of history" was a radical departure from second-Temple Jewish hope.[53] Consequently, although some women in their group announced they were greeted at the empty tomb of Jesus that same morning by an angelic witness to Christ's resurrection, (and in spite of the fact that some of the men in their party had gone to the tomb and verified it was empty), this too was received as just more bad news: "But him they did not see" (Luke 24:22–24).[54]

Beginning with Moses and all of the prophets, the stranger then tells Israel's story to the two disciples, but in a most unexpected way: the disciples had been blind to God's redemptive purposes for Israel and the world through the Messiah's sufferings and vindication (Luke 24:26–27).

Finally, the three of them come to the end of the road and Jesus' astonishing exposition of the whole of Scripture. By now, the sun has begun to set on the first Easter Sunday. It is evening and the two disciples invite the stranger to stay with them (Luke 24:28–29). The evening meal is prepared and served; the stranger takes the bread, gives thanks and breaks it, and "their eyes were opened and they recognized him, and he disappeared from their sight" (Luke 24:30–31).[55]

The structural simplicity of Luke's account makes the Resurrection the *sine qua non* of Israel's story: the Resurrection has liberated God's people, they have been restored from exile, their sins are forgiven and Israel's covenant is renewed with Yahweh![56]

WHAT WAS JESUS FOR ISRAEL?

Jesus was for Israel what they could not be for themselves—although Jesus did not conform to the pharisaic interpretations of the Jewish controlling narrative, he was for Israel their Messiah.

Jesus was for Israel, a new Moses enacting a new Exodus; the multiplication of the loaves and fishes in the austerity of the wilderness is a sign of covenant renewal, the miracle of divine redistribution of God's bounty to a spiritually wandering people, clean and unclean together, points to the end of Israel's exile, the forgiveness of sins and the restoration of the covenant.

Messianic images from Isaiah (25:6–9) are again revealed in the wilderness in a second miraculous wilderness feeding. Many people have come "from far off" indicating the presence of Gentiles among Jews. Jesus extends the covenant to the Gentile world; Gentiles, as well as Jews, are no longer in exile. Inclusion in the kingdom of God is not by means of the Temple cult ritual or ethnic identity but through relationship with God's Messiah, Jesus of Nazareth. The eschatological banquet will include many "from the east and the west" who will sit down with Abraham, Isaac, and Jacob.

Jesus was for Israel a new relationship with God and relationship with Jesus was tantamount to entrance into God's kingdom; however, Jesus' table fellowship was an offense to some, especially to the self-righteous and hypocritical. Consequently, they could not see God's tangible symbol of salvation in Christ. Instead, the offended pious leveled accusations against Jesus: "Here is a glutton and a drunkard."

Jesus was for Israel the revelation of a new political agenda ordered by alternative eschatological expectations. The advent of the kingdom through revolutionary zeal and the national symbols, which had become the focal point of the aforementioned zeal, are replaced by the humility and poverty of the Incarnation.

Jesus' restored-from-exile theology comes together symbolically in the upper room. Jesus' last meal with his disciples climatically points to the fulfillment of Yahweh's kingdom-purposes in himself; Israel will be delivered from their "exilic plight" through Jesus' blood "poured out for many."[57]

Jesus' post-mortem journey from Jerusalem to Emmaus with two of his despairing disciples culminates with the "breaking of the bread" as a central feature of Luke's Easter narrative and the common theme of Jesus' table fellowship throughout the gospels: the future eschatological banquet.

In his commentary on Luke, Ellis "points out that the meal in Emmaus is the eighth meal scene in the gospel, where the Last Supper was the seventh: the week of the first creation is over, Easter is the beginning of the new creation."[58] God has reclaimed his creation in sovereign power through the Resurrection, the old creation is put to death at Calvary and new creation emerges on Easter Sunday—the tomb is the womb of new creation!

WHAT IS THE CHURCH TO BE FOR THE WORLD?

Excluding the three meals in the homes of Pharisees, the sacred symbol of the Eucharist embodies the themes of Christ's other eight meals surveyed in this chapter—the Supper is a symbol of the church's vocation to be for the world what Jesus was for Israel.

The Eucharist is revelation that the church is a new covenant community, and the first-fruits of the new world order (1 Cor. 11:24–25). Whenever the church ingests the bread and the cup, it proclaims Christ's atoning death until He returns a second time—the Eucharist places the church in the context of a realized eschatology[59]: "Despite the discontinuity between the present mode of corruptible physicality and the future world of non-corruptible physicality, there is an underlying continuity between present bodily life and future bodily life, and that gives meaning and direction to present Christian living."[60]

The breaking of the bread tacitly reminds the church that the exiled Christ was broken in body in his passion. Likewise, the church is commissioned in her "present Christian living" to an exilic passion—the church is a sacrament for the culture; and therefore, the church is to be for the world what it cannot be for itself.

The Eucharist reminds the church that God's apocalyptic agenda does not mean the end of the world. The bread and the cup as material elements inform the church that God has reclaimed his creation through Christ's physical, bodily resurrection; creation is being renewed, restored, and recreated.

The church has been reconciled to God through faith in Christ; and the church is to be reconciled to one another. The bread symbolizes the unity of the body of Christ: "There is one loaf, we, who are many, are one body, for we all partake of the one loaf" (1 Cor. 10:17). And the Eucharist symbolizes Christ's restoration eschatology: "Is not the cup of thanksgiving for which we give thanks a participation in the blood of Christ? And is not the bread that we break a participation in the body of Christ?" (1 Cor. 10:16/2 Cor. 5:17-20).

The cup is the new covenant in Christ's blood and the table reminds the repentant church she is separated unto God through faith in Christ, but this does not mean the church is to be separated from the world; she is to be actively involved in divine redistribution—the church is to participate with the eschatological Spirit in making all things new!

Humanity's return from exile is now a present reality. The plainness of the elements call to remembrance the church's spiritual poverty and the church's poverty (spiritual humility) is tangible evidence that the kingdom of God is now open to the world. However, when much of the evangelical church speaks of "the kingdom of God" they often use verbs such as "build the kingdom" or "bring the kingdom" or "advance" or "establish" the kingdom. The kingdom of God is a present reality, "the immediate presence of the Kingdom is found in Jesus."[61] God's inaugural eschatology in Christ informs the church to *implement* Christ's work—rather than "building" or "bringing" the kingdom of God through "works righteousness." *The reality of the present kingdom of God ought to order the political agenda of the church.*

In "the Eucharist, we touch, taste, smell, see and hear a story that enters us as food and drink—a story of a body that was pierced and then glorified."[62] The simple sign of the bread and the cup, their lack of beauty and glory remind the church that Christian praxis in the world is to be marked by the exchanging of wealth (status; access to power) for poverty (spiritual humility) and relocation from the center to the margins—the church's "journey to Burning Man" is the recovery of her vocation.

CONCLUSION—THE CHURCH'S VOCATION: 'A GLUTTON AND A DRUNKARD'

According to N. T. Wright, the church is called,

> to discern where in your discipline the human project is showing signs of exile and humbly and boldly to act symbolically in ways that declare that the powers have been defeated, that the kingdom has come in Jesus the Jewish Messiah, that the new way of being human has been unveiled, and to be prepared to tell the story that explains what these symbols are all about.[63]

For the church to unveil "the new way of being human," it must *Re-Form*—the church must exchange its [external] radical dualistic mindset for a Biblical world-view framed in the unifying themes of Jesus' table-fellowship.[64] The Kingdom has come in Christ—an *inaugural eschatology* means the Kingdom is a present reality. And an inaugural eschatology informs the conscience of the Church that she is the first-fruits of new creation, a new humanity, a new covenant community.

A *restoration eschatology* informs the church of the need to *Re-connect* with culture at the point of contact between a culture's "signs of exile"[65] and the gospel—the church must retell the culture's story in terms of the Jesus story, the gospel, through enactment (social and economic justice) and proclamation (the preaching of the Cross).

A *realized eschatology* places the ministry of the church in a paradoxical context: the kingdom of God now present is the first-fruits of a still future kingdom—"the powers have been defeated"; Christ has reclaimed his creation and he is "making all things new;" the Spirit empowered church is to join Christ in *Re-creating*—wherever a hurting place exists in the local church's community, that is where Jesus will be!

The transformation of England's culture through William Wilberforce's 'Vital Christianity'—the conflation of social justice and the preaching of the Cross—inspires 21st century Christian ministry.

NOTES

1. Discontinuous change is unpredictable, ever-changing and creates insecurity. Discontinuous change is disruptive and unanticipated; it creates situations that challenge our assumptions.

2. My understanding of the church's vocation is an adaptation of N.T. Wright's writing. For example: N.T. Wright, *The Challenge of Jesus* (Downers Grove, IL: Inter-Varsity Press, 1999), 53:

What Jesus was to Israel, the church must now be for the world. Everything we discover about what Jesus did and said within the Judaism of his day must be thought through in terms of what it would look like for the church to do and be for the world. If we are to shape our world, and perhaps even to implement the redemption of our world, this is how it is to be done.

Also, Wright, page 181, *The Challenge of Jesus,* reflects this thought as well. The prolific British Bishop uses this phraseology and many other thoughts that have profoundly shaped my thinking throughout many of his books and articles.

3. Jim Wallis, *God's Politics* (San Francisco: Harper, 2005), 34–35.

4. Ibid.

5. "Radical dualism" is used in this chapter to describe the church's *external* sense of the need to draw sharp lines of demarcation between sacred and secular, the church and the world, Christ and culture. Descartes' western ontological dualism, the sharp distinction between "physical" and "spiritual" or "material" and "non-material," i.e., an externally radical dualism, would be alien to Paul and his original audiences.

6. Allen Lewis, *Between Cross & Resurrection, A Theology of Holy Saturday* (Grand Rapids, MI: William B. Eerdmans, 2001), 124.

7. See N. T. Wright, *The New Testament and the People of God* (Minneapolis: Fortress Press, 1992), PART III: First-Century Judaism within the Greco-Roman World, 145–279 for full discussion of Israel's controlling narrative during the Second Temple Period.

8. N. T. Wight, *Jesus and the Victory of God* (Minneapolis: Fortress Press, 1996), 255. See also, Craig Blomberg, *Contagious Holiness, Jesus' Meals With Sinners* (Downers Grove, IL: Inter-Varsity Press, 2005), 102 and Marcus Borg, *Conflict, Holiness, and Politics in the Teaching of Jesus* (New York: Mellon, 1984), 135. The requirement of repentance before entering the kingdom of God is consistent with Jesus' message, e.g., Matthew 4:17.

9. C. T. McMahan, "Meals As Type-Scenes in the Gospel of Luke" (PhD diss., Southern Baptist Theological Seminary, 1987), 1, quoted in Craig Blomberg, *Contagious Holiness, Jesus' Meals With Sinners*, 163.

10. The subversive character of Jesus' table-fellowship, including a broad cross section of people in the Synoptic tradition, satisfies the multiple attestation criteria for the authenticity of the texts surveyed in chapter 2. The meals of Jesus also satisfy the criterion of dissimilarity, Jesus' eating with sinners is unique in the ancient Palestinian context. Further, Jesus' table-fellowship coheres with his teaching throughout the gospel narratives about the kingdom of God.

In addition to the standard criteria including multiple attestation, dissimilarity, Palestinian context, and coherence, Wright further calls for a "double similarity and dissimilarity." He writes, "When something can be seen to be credible (though perhaps deeply subversive) within first-century Judaism, and credible as the implied starting point (though not the exact replica) of something in later Christianity, there is a strong possibility of our being in touch with the genuine history of Jesus.". Satisfaction of the criterion of double similarity and dissimilarity dispels notions that a saying could have been the product of the later church rather than original.

The meal motif in the gospels remains a conspicuous feature of Christian fellowship everywhere and in every age. More specifically, the primitive Christian Church continued "the breaking of bread" together as a central part of their faith in Jesus (Acts 2:42). Paul's words in his first letter to the Corinthians (11:23–26) recall the church's sacred tradition and practice of the Eucharist: "For I received from the Lord what I also passed onto you."

The wedding feast of the Lamb is a glorious picture of Jesus' table-fellowship outside the gospel tradition. The redeemed from every age, tongue, ethnicity, and nationality will come together as the Bride of Christ to share in the wedding banquet prepared for them by their Lord at the end of the age (Rev. 19:7–9).

11. A few scholars have argued that the festive character of Jesus' table-fellowship evinces a Greco-Roman form of banqueting referred to as symposium. Symposia included a formal meal eaten by people reclining on couches. The meal was followed by the drinking of wine, discussion of a variety of controversial topics musical entertainment, and often sexual exploitation. Blomberg debunks the claim that symposia had become ubiquitous in first-century Jewish culture. He contends, for example, the messianic banquet is consumed while being seated as opposed to reclining. The biblical tradition consistently portrays those eating a formal meal sitting. Whereas the "breaking of bread" was an important role assumed by the father in Jewish circles, this had no significance in the Greco-Roman symposia. The Jews were concerned with ceremonial cleanliness and the Greeks were not. *Contagious Holiness*, 84, 94–95.

12. Blomberg notes that Semitic as well as Greek constructions sometimes allow for one noun form such as "tax collectors" to be a subset for the others such as "sinners." Nevertheless, Matthew and his friends are viewed as corrupt beyond the general immorality ascribed to Jews living under Roman occupation. Ibid., 99.

13. Blomberg notes the verb *idontes* translated "saw" in Mark 2:16 may simply mean "finding out." Ibid., 100.

14. Ben Witherington III, *The Gospel of Mark: A Socio-Rhetorical Commentary* (Grand Rapids, MI: William B. Eerdmans, 2001), 123.

15. Blomberg, *Contagious Holiness,* 100. Luke's parallel account (5:27–32) informs asserts Levi "left everything" (v. 28) to follow Jesus.

16. Mark had made implicit what Luke makes explicit: "I have not come to call the righteous but sinners to repentance" (Luke 5:32).

17. Christ's "impoverished state" refers to 2 Corinthians 8:9: "For you know the grace of our Lord Jesus Christ, that though he was rich, yet for your sakes he became poor, so that you through his poverty might become rich."

18. Matthew 9:36 refers to Jesus' compassion for the crowds who were like sheep without a shepherd. Jesus tells parables about lost sheep and a shepherd and a shepherd with sheep and goats (Matt 18:1–14; Luke 15:3–7). Jesus refers to Himself as the good Shepherd in John 10:11. Mark and Matthew place Zechariah 13:7, "strike the shepherd, and the sheep will be scattered," on Jesus' lips.

19. Wright remarks, "Negatively, this covenant renewal meant judgment falling on the nation: the parable of Luke 13:6–9 (the fig tree that eventually bears no fruit)

becomes an acted parable in Matthew 21.18–20/Mark 11.12–25, where it clearly symbolizes the same as the action in the Temple, i.e., the imminent judgment that will fall on impenitent Israel," *Jesus and the Victory of God,* 193.

20. W. L. Lane, *The Gospel According to Mark* (Grand Rapids, MI: William B. Eerdmans, 1974), 232–233.

21. Blomberg, Contagious Holiness, 106.

22. J. B. Green, *The Gospel of Luke* (Grand Rapids, MI: William B. Eerdmans, 1997), 365.

23. Witherington, *The Gospel of Mark*, 235–236.

24. Jesus appears to place himself on the same level as John the Baptist, a notion the primitive church would have rejected; this point supports textual authenticity. Also, the slander, "glutton and a drunkard," against Jesus by his critics would most certainly have been offensive to the later church.

25. The accusation, "glutton and drunkard" appears to be a reference to the "rebellious son" who was worthy of death under Old Testament Law (Deut 13:17, Prov 23:19–21; 28:7).

26. This is evidence of Jesus' intention to celebrate this meal with "sinners" as an enactment of the messianic banquet.

27. The wrongness of this rejection will become evident when "wisdom is vindicated." The motif recalls both Wisdom 2 and 5, whose rejected and vindicated protagonist is the spokesman of Wisdom, and the Parables of Enoch, whose exalted protagonist has some of the characteristics of preexistent Wisdom. Paradoxically, the son of man's ministry is characterized by the reconciliation of sinners." *Anchor Bible Dictionary*, W.E. George Nickelsburg, "Son of Man," Vol. 6, ed. David Noel Freedman (New York: Doubleday), 137–150.

28. David Seccombe, The King of God's Kingdom: A Solution to the Puzzle of Jesus (Carlisle, UK: Paternoster, 2002), 240.

29. Bonnie L. Pattison, Poverty in the Theology of John Calvin, 151.

30. Wright, Jesus and the Victory of God, 149.

31. Concerning the woman's spiritual condition, Blomberg notes: "The woman need not be a prostitute. The other possibilities are that she is the wife of someone with a dishonorable occupation . . . a woman in debt, or an adulteress." Blomberg, *Contagious Holiness*, 132. Additionally, observes Barbara Reid, the woman could have been ill, disabled, or she could have had frequent contact with Gentiles, "'Do You See This Woman?" Luke 7:36–50 as a Paradigm for Feminist Hermeneutics." *BR* 40: 37–49, quoted in Blomberg, *Contagious Holiness*, 132.

32. Ibid., 134.

33. Matthew 23:1–39 reveals a litany of woes leveled by Jesus against the Pharisees. The Matthean parallel does not place Jesus in the Pharisee's home for a meal.

34. R. Stein observes that the ceremonial cleansing has to do with oral Torah, not any written requirement in the Hebrew Scriptures, see *Luke* (Nashville, TN: Broadman Press, 1992), 340.

35. Blomberg, Contagious Holiness, 143.

36. Ibid., 144.

37. Dropsy was a disease contracted by people who drank too much. The symptoms were a bloated condition and an unquenchable thirst.

38. Stein, *Luke*, 392.
39. Wright, Jesus and the Victory of God, 390.
40. Blomberg, Contagious Holiness, 148.
41. Ibid., 394–395.
42. Blomberg observes the imperfect tense of *zeteo*, which suggests continual or ongoing seeking on Zacchaeus' part. *Contagious Holiness*, 152. Blomberg's aforementioned observation is cause to wonder why Luke does not explain Zaccheaus was so determined to see Jesus.
43. I. Howard Marshall, *The Gospel of Luke* (Grand Rapids, MI: William B. Eerdmans, 1978), 697.
44. Ibid.
45. Wright, Jesus and the Victory of God, 257.
46. Wright observes that John "indicates that the meal took place the day *before* the feast; he does not, however, describe the meal, or any symbolic actions concerned with the bread and wine, but only the footwashing (Jn. 13.1; 18.28; 19.14.31.) This fits with the Talmudic evidence, which had Jesus being executed 'on the eve of the Passover' (bSand. 43a.) Various attempts have been made to resolve this problem. Jesus may have been following a rival (perhaps Essene?) calendar; John has altered the chronology to make the theological point that Jesus is the true Passover lamb, slaughtered at the same time as the lambs were being killed in the Temple in preparation for the evening meal; the synopists have turned the meal into a Passover meal in obedience to *their* theology or tradition." Ibid., 555.
47. The *Hallel* Psalms are 115–118.
48. Wright, Jesus and the Victory of God, 560.
49. Jesus' words and actions are linked to His disruptive actions in the Temple. Jesus' cessation of the daily sacrifice and the normal business otherwise transacted during the time of the Passover was symbolic of the Temple's destruction which would take place within a generation. See Wright, *Jesus and the Victory of God*, 413–428 for a full explanation of the significance of Jesus' actions in the Temple.
50. N. T. Wright, "The Resurrection and the Postmodern Dilemma," N. T. Wright Page, http://www.ntwrightpage.com/Wright_Resurrection_Postmodern.htm (09/25/05).
51. Evangelicals and progressives together agree that the only sufficient explanation for the rise of Christianity is Jesus' resurrection. See, for example, Marcus Borg and N.T. Wright, *The Meaning of Jesus, Two Visions* (San Francisco: Harper, 1998), 129.
52. See especially Isaiah 40–55 where Jewish eschatological expectations, and in particular these motifs, emerge.
53. N. T. Wright, *The Resurrection of the Son of God* (Minneapolis: Fortress Press, 2003), 415.
54. Would not the reader of this story have just cause to suspect its veracity if the two despairing disciples, most probably husband and wife, have immediately recognized Jesus of Nazareth? This is not to mention the entire company's skepticism in the face of the women's report, see Luke 24:9–11.
55. The Jewish controlling narrative's concealment rather than the illumination of the advent of the Messiah caused Jesus' disciples great distress and fear when the risen Lord appeared, post-mortem, to them, Luke 24:36–39. This point is relevant to

the issue of the historicity of this text and the "everything or nothing" importance of the Resurrection to the symbolic world of the gospel.

56. Isaiah 26:16–21; 40:1–11, Jeremiah 31:31–41, Ezekiel 36:22–32; 37:1–1, and Daniel 9; 12:2.

57. Former Jewish washings are replaced by the "new wine" of Jesus' life for God's covenant people. Christ's final Passover meal with his disciples marks the dawning of a new age; "all nations will be blessed" through the new Exodus and Israel's Messiah.

58. N.T. Wright, "The Resurrection and the Postmodern Dilemma," 8.

59. The collapsing of the church's realized eschatology; the breaking of the tension between present realization and future hope, invokes the sense of a kingdom in the present as opposed to a future kingdom. The consequence of this broken tension inevitably leads to a dualism in the church's mindset and her uncritical substitution of a realized eschatology for a vertical eschatology. Consequently, the church's focus is on private piety and a corresponding world-denying social critique. In practical terms, the church's radical dualism keeps her light within, increasing the sense of personal purity, political power, and exclusiveness while leaving the culture in darkness.

60. Wright, The Resurrection of the Son of God, 359.

61. Jules Glanzer, quoted in Leonard Sweet, *The Three Hardest Words in the World to Get Right* (New York: Waterbrook, 2006), 31.

62. Andy Crouch, "Life After Postmodernity," in *The Church in Emerging Culture*, ed. Leonard Sweet (Grand Rapids, MI: Zondervan, 2003), 85.

63. Wright, The Challenge of Jesus, 187.

64. The Barna Group, "Barna Survey Examines Changes in Worldview Among Christians over the Past 13 Years," March 6, 2009, reports that less than 1 in 5, 19%, of born-again Christians think in terms of a biblical world-view. Christians, clergy and lay-persons' mindset, is largely shaped by modernity; modernism is the source of the external radical dualism (ontological dualism) characteristic of many contemporary Christians.

65. N.T. Wright, The Challenge of Jesus, 174–197.

Chapter Three

William Wilberforce and "Vital Christianity"

William Wilberforce (1759–1833) was a principled politician, a Christian statesman whose uncompromising convictions enabled him to transcend party lines for the sake of the common good of society. In his cultural apologetic, *A Practical View of Christianity*, Wilberforce writes, "If indeed through the blessing of Providence, a principle of true Religion should in any considerable degree gain ground, there is no estimating the effects on public morals, and the consequent influence on our political welfare."[1] In extremely difficult times marked by war, moral decay, and political polarization, Wilberforce boldly called upon the British Empire to embrace "Vital Christianity."

VITAL CHRISTIANITY

Wilberforce and his Christian community, the Clapham Group, were committed to "the practical expression of the Christian faith in self-sacrificial giving of themselves, in time, energy, and money for the relief of poverty, for the care of the distressed, for the dispelling of ignorance, for the preaching of the gospel both at home and overseas, for setting the captives free and combating exploitation."[2] The Clapham Sect took Jesus' command seriously to show compassion to all human beings, to "visit the sick and the prisoners, to feed the hungry and clothe the naked, for inasmuch as they did it to the least of humanity they were doing it to the Lord."[3] The conflation of the proclamation of the gospel and social and economic justice is Vital Christianity, a "true Religion."

Wilberforce and the Clapham Community's Vital Christianity is an inspiring historic picture of how: (1) social reform is an essential part of people's willingness to hear the gospel; (2) the Spirit-filled life is not about withdrawing from the culture, but believers immersing themselves in it and transforming it from within; (3) the local church can transform culture by inspiring believers to take social and political responsibility seriously as an essential part of sharing the gospel of Jesus Christ; and (4) Wilberforce and the Clapham Sect's grassroots political philosophy effectively forced the British Parliament to support their moral-ethical reforms.

This chapter addresses how individuals whose lives have been transformed by the power of the gospel can transform their culture. Vital Christianity is a timely and meaningful contribution to the church's recovery of its vocation in the twenty-first-century context. The "great change" in the life of "the shrimp" who led Parliament to abolish slavery in Great Britain and the colonies was the source of his perseverance, courage and compassion.

CHRISTIAN SINGULARITY

Wilberforce began his political career in Commons representing his home district of Hull in 1780; however, he represented Yorkshire, England's most powerful county, for the greater part of his political career in Parliament (1784–1825). His political life was defined by his conversion to Christian faith.

Wilberforce came to faith through a gradual process lasting from October 1784 through Easter 1786. His journey to salvation began with a continental tour he planned to take with his mother, sister, and other family members. He desired a learned companion to accompany him for the purpose of extended dialogue throughout the trip. He invited Dr. William Burgh of York, a scholarly man whom he had known for many years to be his companion, but Burgh was unable to go. In Burgh's place, Wilberforce asked Isaac Milner, a respected Cambridge don.

Milner was an evangelical Christian who, in Wilberforce's words, persuasively set forth "the intellectual heart of Christianity."[4] Prior to asking Milner to be his traveling companion, Wilberforce was unaware of his former tutor's deep Christian convictions; and had he been aware of them, he would not have asked Milner to accompany him.[5]

At this time in his life, in spite of extended exposure to Methodism in his childhood while in the care of his aunt and uncle following his father's untimely death, Wilberforce was a religious skeptic. However, the evangelical Christian faith of his aunt and uncle began returning to Wilberforce's life during his tour of continental Europe. As they traveled together, Milner and Wilberforce read and discussed the Greek New Testament. They also engaged in conversation about a book that would profoundly set Wilberforce on his journey towards his "Great Change," *The Rise and Progress of Religion in the Soul* by Philip Doddridge (1701–1751).[6]

Wilberforce's discussions with Milner brought him to a settled conviction in his mind of "the truth of Christianity."[7] His Christian faith would become the all-consuming source of his political career and his incomparable achievements in behalf of humanity, in Britain and throughout the earth. In Wilberforce, the presumed incompatible characters of statesman and Christian coincided to God's glory and humanity's great benefit.[8]

In 1787, two years after his conversion to Christianity, Wilberforce penned the concentration of his deepest convictions: "God Almighty has set before me two great objects: the suppression of the slave trade and the reformation of manners."[9]

Wilberforce's indomitable spirit, "the friend of Africa," drove him in his unrelenting perseverance: "The pathway to abolition was fraught with difficulty. Vested interest, parliamentary filibustering, entrenched bigotry, international politics, slave unrest, personal sickness, and political fear—all combined to frustrate the movement."[10]

On February 23, 1807, after twenty years of unrelenting criticism, threats on his life, stubborn prejudice on the part of his colleagues in Parliament, and a serious illness in 1788 that almost claimed Wilberforce's life, a Bill for the Abolition of the Slave Trade was passed in the House by a vote of 283 to 16.[11]

After another twenty-six years of enduring political, social, and spiritual battles the Emancipation Bill abolishing slavery in all of the British colonies passed in Parliament on July 26, 1833. Three days later, following forty-six years of steadfast faith in the face of overwhelming odds, Wilberforce died.

"A principle of true Religion" was for Wilberforce a Vital Christianity and Christian Singularity, contrary to a nominal Christianity, is committed both to the unashamed proclamation of the gospel and the common good of humanity. Wilberforce's Vital Christianity was centered in two great theological emphases: restoration eschatology (the finished work of Christ) and the Spirit's eschatological work.

Wilberforce stood with Charles Simeon in his profound belief that an evangelical Christian was one who "determined not to know anything among you save Jesus Christ and him crucified."[12] The Holy Spirit was essential to both personal salvation and the spiritual growth and vitality of the believers: "This emphasis upon the activity of the Spirit most obviously differentiated evangelicals' beliefs from those of their fellows."[13]

The British reformer equally stressed the value of good works for faith without works is dead (James 2:14–26). Vital Christianity is committed to the common good of the culture by its unashamed, single-minded commitment to the Cross, and the dynamic power of the Holy Spirit's presence in the lives of believers.[14]

Wilberforce conceived of society as divinely designed hierarchically and organically; the different parts of culture work together according to their divinely appointed role and leaders guide and rule this process and serve the needs of the poor (who also had a role in society defined by God). Wilberforce's vision for society was for Christian faith to be "carried into every corner of life and allowed to fill it."[15]

VITAL CHRISTIANITY AND CULTURAL TRANSFORMATION

In opposition to the social liberal gospel, many contemporary evangelicals have chosen cultural isolation (an external dualistic mindset). The Clapham Sect's Vital Christianity implores the church to abandon her former either/or commitments to social action and/or personal salvation and unite these two expressions of Christianity.

Cultural transformation proceeds from a transformed church. The "radical benefit of restoring the influence of Religion," is the raising of "the standard of morality."[16] The transformed church discerns the presence of the kingdom of God everywhere in the cosmos but in clear distinction from the world system.[17] Hill writes:

> A change of mindset in the church is required to move from seeing the local church as the centre of community in a neighborhood setting, to seeing the church in missional terms as the equipper and enabler of believers who have a mission in wider society. The local church ... may continue to be a worshipping community, but its prime function must move from being an end in itself to being a resource agency for mission. This requires fundamental change from the local church having its prime purpose of meeting the needs of its congregation and serving the local community through the provision of facilities for meetings and community activities, to one of embracing the Great Commission ... and adjusting its sights from inward-looking to outward-looking, from local community development to wider mission. We have to stop thinking in terms of local church growth as an end in itself. The prime objective of the Christian faith is not to build the church as a great institution but to evangelize the world![18]

The [bodily] Resurrection, God's reaffirmation of the goodness of His creation, constitutes the Divine will for the church to engage in culture's redemption. Whereas there is no blueprint for cultural transformation, prudent application of the broad contours and principles of Wilberforce's Vital Christianity will significantly fund societal redemption in any age. Five principles for cultural transformation, following from Vital Christianity, begin with the power of community through the reconciliation and unity of the church.

BUILDING COMMUNITY

Michael Green describes the church as the new humanity, the first-fruits of God's providential renewing of all creation:

> They made the grace of God credible by a society of love and mutual care which astonished pagans and was recognized as something entirely new. It lent persuasiveness to the claim that the new age had dawned in those who were giving it flesh. The message of the kingdom became more than an idea. A new human community had sprung up and looked very much like the new order to which the evangelist had pointed. Here love was given daily expression; reconciliation was actually occurring; people were no longer divided into Jews and Gentiles, slave and free, male and female. In this community the weak were protected, the stranger welcomed. People were healed, the poor and dispossessed were cared for and found justice. Almost everything was shared. Joy abounded and ordinary lives were filled with praise.[19]

The character and commitment of the primitive Christian community was re-birthed in Wilberforce and the Clapham group, a collection of politicians, churchmen, lawyers, merchants, bankers, and poets who together called for the moral reform of British society and the abolition of the slave trade. The Clapham community infused social action with Vital Christianity and dynamically transformed not only a nation, but significant portions of the world.

> Because of the Clapham Sect, England's policies and England's actions became more humane and more enlightened. Indeed, Clapham influence extended beyond England. Spain, Portugal, France, Holland, Sweden, Russia, and, at the international conferences, still other countries, were led by pressure from Clapham to actions they would not otherwise have taken. No peace negotiations, no council of the period, escaped the influence of the Clapham Sect. Amiens, Paris, Vienna, Aixla-Chapelle, and Verona were all bombarded by Clapham letters and Clapham pamphlets; and sometimes persuaded by speeches and documents carefully planned by the Clapham "Cabinet Councils," and painstakingly drafted by Clapham labourers.[20]

Besides Wilberforce, the Clapham Saints included: Henry Thornton (1760–1815) a banker, philanthropist and member of parliament; John Venn (1799–1813), rector of Clapham Parish Church; Thomas Babington (1758–1837), banker, philanthropist and abolitionist; Thomas Clarkson (1760–1846), abolitionist, and researcher; Charles Grant (1746–1823), chairman and director of the East India Company and member of parliament; Zachary Macaulay (1768–1838), governor of Sierra Leone and editor of the *Christian Observer*, a monthly evangelical Christian periodical; Isaac Milner (1750–1820), an academic and member of the Royal Society; Hannah More (1745–1833), writer and educationist; Granville Sharpe (1735–1813), philanthropist and abolitionist; Charles Simeon (1759–1836), vicar of Holy Trinity, Cambridge; James Stephen (1758–1832), lawyer, member of parliament and abolitionist; John Shore (1751–1834), governor general of India and president of the Bible Society; John Thornton (1720–1790), merchant and philanthropist; Henry Venn (1724–1797), vicar of Huddersfield and Yelling; John Newton (1725–1807), evangelical Anglican clergyman and hymn writer and William Cowper (1731–1800), poet, hymn writer, and curate to John Newton.

A total of thirty members in the Commons, among them were members of both the Whigs and the Tory Parties, were included in the Clapham Sect. Later, following Wilberforce's retirement from Parliament in 1825, several evangelical Christians who were of one mind with the Clapham Sect entered Parliament. They came together with remaining members of the Clapham Saints in Parliament to achieve the final abolition of slavery just days before Wilberforce's death in 1833. Between 1780 and 1840, more evangelical Christians were elected to the House of Commons; they continued in the cause of Christ and the Clapham Community.[21]

Hill observes that one of the remarkable things about the Clapham Saints was "the balance of professional skills and experience within the group. They were lawyers, bankers, churchmen, researchers, politicians and businessmen. Most of them were laymen, but they were all deeply committed Christians who were not just content with merely having a personal faith in God but who needed to express their faith in action."[22]

For the presence of Christ to be "carried into every corner of life and allowed to fill it," a redeemed community of men and women representing "every corner of life" need to unite in the power of God's Spirit and conscientiously commit to the subversion of a given society's systemic ills through their enactment and proclamation of the gospel of Christ.

CONTEXTUALIZING THE GOSPEL

Wilberforce and the Clapham Community collectively used their resources and positions in society to achieve their mission. They came "from every corner of life" for the purpose of taking Christ to every corner of life and filling it with his presence.

> The Clapham Sect, the leading Evangelicals of their day, did not divorce religion from life. They linked religion to life. They linked it to the hunted Negroes on the coast of Africa, on the high seas, and in the plantations of the West Indies. They linked it to standards of political conduct, the corrupt manners of society, and to the debauched mobs of their time. They linked it to the wretches condemned by game laws, and oppressed in filthy prisons. They linked it to the ragged children condemned otherwise to ignorance, and by philanthropic and benefit societies they linked it to the improvident and unfortunate poor.[23]

In an age when politicians and most church leaders were oblivious to the real source of societal ills, the Clapham Sect linked the gospel to the poverty of Christ. Through Christ's compassion and empathy, the Clapham Community related the gospel to the deepest longings of each "corner of life."

The common people heard the message preached by Wesley and Whitefield a generation earlier, but the upper class rejected what they saw as emotionalism and they resented being confronted by news of their personal depravity. The ranks of the Clapham sect included men and women representative of upper class society. The Clapham Group built on the foundations laid by Wesley and Whitefield and brought the gospel to Parliament and professional and commercial spheres throughout Great Britain.

The Clapham Group's Vital Christianity produced a "new evangelicalism" by conflating the gospel proclaimed by the revivalists with compassionate reforming social action; the Clapham sect brought the center and the margins together through the dynamic of the gospel.

> In fact Evangelicalism played here a role similar to that which it has played in all the humanitarian movements of modern England. It constituted a link, effected the transition between Anglicanism and Dissent, between the governing classes and the general public, as represented by the great middle-class. It prevented the formation of a reactionary group and won the support of the gentry and nobility, sometimes even of a member of the Royal Family, for a movement initiated by shopkeepers and preachers. And the action of the party was decisive in securing from Parliament the legislation which embodied the dictates of the national conscience.[24]

The contextualizing of the gospel in every "corner of life," beginning with Wesley and Whitefield and concluding with the "new evangelicalism" of the Clapham sect laid the foundations for the Victorian era in the next generation, an age of manners and civility.

THE COMMON GOOD

The Clapham Community held in common a profound sense of their moral responsibility of stewardship over the many resources God had blessed them with; their strong convictions led them to take Jesus literally and love the very least of humanity for in this they were caring for Christ.

The Clapham Sect was committed to the infusion of justice, compassion and Christian standards of morality into society. They were more focused on the moral and spiritual condition of the general populace than on sweeping political reforms. Thus, the transformation of the British culture was sustained over time largely because the Clapham reforms were grassroots and, therefore, they were embraced by people of every socio-economic class. Consequently, societal transformation in England was not dependent on the church, political parties or cultural institutions.

The Clapham ethos was marked by the group's giving to and participation in numerous charitable societies. They turned their belief into practice and, consequently, anyone associated with the Clapham Sect was widely known for their commitment to personal evangelism and social and economic justice to include caring for the poor, ministering to the sick and the dying, and founding schools and colleges. They visited the imprisoned and founded philanthropic societies for the welfare of children, orphans, women, the blind, deaf, dumb, and paralytics. The Clapham Sect was committed to the relieving of all human suffering.[25]

Wilberforce belonged to some seventy different philanthropic causes, some he founded himself including the British and Foreign Bible Society (for the spread of the gospel throughout the British colonies), the Society for Bettering the Condition of the Poor (The "Bettering Society" was founded in Wilberforce's home), the Society for the Reformation of Manners, and the Climbing Boy Society (aiding and protecting through legislative sanctions children employed as chimney sweeps). He was an active supporter of other causes such as reforming the penal code, the humanizing of the English criminal code, and to others he was a generous donor including education for the poor and the deaf.[26]

CO-BELLIGERENCE

Wilberforce and Thornton's strategy for cultural transformation involved their use of "co-belligerents" to achieve their objectives. Vital Christianity acknowledges individuals cannot change the times alone, they need co-belligerent relationships to achieve objectives for the common good. Co-belligerent relationships involve partnering with others who may not necessarily share the political philosophy, values, or beliefs of Christians but share personal convictions and concerns on particular moral/ethical matters.

Wilberforce and the Clapham Community were not afraid of damaging their personal integrity by enlisting others committed to their goals, reforms, and projects. On a certain occasion, Wilberforce counseled his son Samuel: "Never omit any opportunity of getting acquainted with any good man or any useful man."[27] Wilberforce applied the principle, "measures, not men" as he worked with philosophical opposites to achieve an array of objectives from abolition to prison reform.

POLITICAL PHILOSOPHY

In a letter to William Cowper, John Newton said of Wilberforce: "I judge he is now decidedly on the right track. . . . I hope the Lord will make him a blessing both as a Christian and a statesman. How seldom do these characters coincide!! But they are not incompatible."[28] Many of Wilberforce's friends and parliamentary colleagues, however, believed these two characters to be quite incompatible; at times Wilberforce appeared to them to be more a "glutton and a drunkard" than a man in pursuit of God's heart.

Wilberforce, over the long course of his career, faithfully displayed the compatibility of the roles of Christian and statesmen through his integration of faith, reform, political leadership, and the consequent transformation of British society. Wilberforce forcefully expressed his heart on the matter in his *A Practical View of Christianity*:

> Let it be remembered, that the grand characteristic mark of the true Christian, which has been insisted on, is *desiring to please God in all his thoughts, and words, and actions; to take the revealed word to be the rule of his belief and practice; to "Let his light shine before men"; and in all things to adorn the doctrine which he professes*. No calling is proscribed, no pursuit is forbidden, no science or art, no pleasure is disallowed, which is reconcilable with this principle.[29]

British politics were skeptical and hostile towards evangelical Christian faith, but Wilberforce was not intimidated by this opposition. Following after Paul's example in Athens viz., the Apostle's confrontation of the prominent Greek philosophers, William Wilberforce consistently employed the literature and philosophy of his day to make his point and advance the cause of Christ. Wilberforce's wise apologetic brought credibility and respectability to the crucial role of religion in society.

The Clapham Community's objective was to change the mindset of the nation towards Christian faith and once again "make goodness fashionable," particularly among the upper classes who admired immorality.

Inspired by the "Golden Rule," William Wilberforce, "the conscience of the nation," contended: "If any country were indeed filled with men, each thus diligently discharging the duties of his own station without breaking in upon the rights of others, but on the contrary endeavoring, so far as he might be able, to forward their views and promote their happiness, all would be active and harmonious in the goodly frame of human society."[30] The four pillars of Wilberforce's political philosophy are set forth in this passage: conscientious stewardship; respect for the rights of others; advancing the views of others and the promotion of the happiness of others.

Regarding stewardship, Wilberforce stressed each individual is endowed by God with "means and occasions . . . of improving ourselves, or of promoting the happiness of others."[31] The conscientious stewardship of God's blessings upon individuals is to be used for the common good of society. This is a sacred duty for all people, especially Christians.

The grounds for every philanthropic and human rights issue is the Golden Rule in Wilberforce's political philosophy. The second political pillar, therefore, the respect for the rights of others, requires "every one to regulate his conduct by the golden rule of doing to others as in similar circumstances we would have them do to us; and the path of duty will be clear before him, and I will add, the decision of [a] legislature would scarcely any longer be doubtful."[32]

Promoting the views of others, the third of Wilberforce's political ideals, involves the practical application of the Golden Rule: place the views of others before the self—hear with understanding what is in the hearts of other people.

Wilberforce's fourth political strategy is the promotion of the happiness of others. Whereas Jefferson's ideal was the personal "pursuit of happiness," Wilberforce believed it was better to promote the happiness of others; indeed this would serve to promote one's own happiness in fuller, more meaningful ways.

Wilberforce and the Clapham Sects' political philosophy was grassroots. The Clapham community's strategy involved extensive field research among the general populace for the purpose of discovering ways and means of relating to society's deepest longings and meeting their needs. The conscience of the nation was moved by the Clapham Groups' unselfishness and compassion and consequently, there was a groundswell of support. This forced the hand of Parliament to pass the Clapham Community's reforms.

These thoroughly Christian political ideals significantly contribute to the harmony of pluralistic society and international relations.

> Such would be the happy state of a truly Christian nation within itself. Nor would its condition with regard to foreign countries form a contrast to this, its internal comfort. Such a community, on the contrary, peaceable at home, would be respected and beloved abroad. General integrity in all its dealings would

inspire universal confidence: differences between nations commonly arise from mutual injuries, and still more from mutual jealousy and distrust. Of the former there would be no longer any ground for complaint; the latter would find nothing to attach upon. But if, in spite of all its justice and forbearance, the violence of some neighboring state should force it to resist an unprovoked attack, for hostilities strictly defensive are those only in which it would be engaged, its domestic union would double its national force, while the consciousness of a good cause, and of the general favor of Heaven, would invigorate its arm, and inspirit its efforts.[33]

In every way, Wilberforce faithfully lived out his Christian convictions, daily applying his political philosophy. Fittingly, Wilberforce's epitaph in Westminster Abbey speaks of "the abiding eloquence of a Christian life."

Wilberforce was a political Independent. He transcended party differences to unite, rather than polarize, the major political parties. The Tory party and the Whigs, as abovementioned, were both represented in the Clapham Community. It was said of Wilberforce, "Not one nation, but the whole human family participated in the benefit he conferred on his fellow men."[34] Wilberforce, however, humbly acknowledged his dependence on God: "His grace is all-sufficient to keep us in any situation which His providence appoints us."[35]

By God's all-sufficient grace in Christ, William Wilberforce and the Clapham Group were for Great Britain and much of the world what Jesus was for Israel. Chapter 4 presents a mosaic of what Vital Christianity may look like in twenty-first-century postmodern culture.

NOTES

1. William Wilberforce, *A Practical View of Christianity* (Peabody, MA: Hendrickson, 1996), 229.
2. Clifford Hill, *The Wilberforce Connection* (Oxford, UK, Monarch, 2004), 139.
3. Ibid.
4. Kevin Belmonte, *William Wilberforce, A Hero of Humanity* (Grand Rapids, MI: Zondervan, 2007), 71.
5. Ibid.
6. Ibid., 74–75.
7. Ibid., 77.
8. Ibid., 87.
9. David J. Vaughan, Statesman and Saint: The Principled Politics of William Wilberforce (Nashville, TN: Highland, 2002), 61.
10. Christopher D. Hancock, "The Shrimp Who Stopped Slavery," *Christian History* 53, (1997): 17.
11. David J. Vaughan, Statesman and Saint: The Principled Politics of William Wilberforce, 93.

12. Doreen M. Rosman, *Evangelicals and Culture* (London: Croom Helm, 1984), 10.

13. Murray Andrew Pura, *Vital Christianity* (Toronto, ONT: Clements, 2003), 11–12.

14. Vital Christianity ought not to be confused with liberal Christianity's "social gospel." The social gospel equates the kingdom of God with social revitalization. Wilberforce clearly believed that the displacing of the Cross with social revitalization as the end of the gospel was anathema.

15. Robin Furneaux, *William Wilberforce* (London: Hamish Hamilton, 1974), 41.

16. Wilberforce, A Practical View of Christianity, 273.

17. C. H. Dodd writes, "When Paul spoke of 'the world' in a moral sense, he was thinking of the totality of people, social systems, values, and traditions in terms of its opposition to God and his redemptive purposes." Quoted in Ronald J. Sider, *The Scandal of the Evangelical Conscience*, 79.

18. Hill, The Wilberforce Connection, 359.

19. Michael Green, quoted in Tom Sine, *Mustard Seed Versus McWorld* (Grand Rapids, MI: Baker, 1999), 205.

20. Ernest Marshall Howse, *Saints in Polities: The Clapham Sect and the Growth of Freedom* (London: George Allen and Unwin, 1952), 177.

21. See Hill, *The Wilberforce Connection*, 19–43, for a brief biography of the Clapham Saints and a listing of later members in Parliament who contributed to the abolition of the slave trade in Great Britain and the colonies.

22. Ibid., 63.

23. Howse, Saints in Polities, 132–33.

24. Elie Halvey, England in 1815, vol. 1 of A History of the English People in the 19th Century (London: Ernest Benn, 1949), 166.

25. Hill, The Wilberforce Connection, 136.

26. Ibid.

27. Belmonte, William Wilberforce, 95.

28. Ibid., 87.

29. Wilberforce, A Practical View of Christianity, 220.

30. Ibid., 221.

31. Belmonte, William Wilberforce, 177.

32. Ibid.

33. Wilberforce, A Practical View of Christianity, 221–22.

34. Belmonte, William Wilberforce, 19.

35. Wilberforce, A Practical View of Christianity, 288.

Chapter Four

Journeying to Burning Man: Recovering the Church's Vocation

A wide canvas banner stretched across the four lanes of the main boulevard leading into my community boldly calls for the 53,000 residents to "Celebrate Diversity!"[1] The postmodern spirit behind the banner invites the diverse population of my progressive university community to participate in a constellation of "realities"—pluralism is an ideology, not merely an observed social phenomenon where I live and minister. Consequently, truth flows from the perspective of a particular community's "interpretative conceptual scheme;" the narrative they create for themselves is their own private reality.

My community is described as a "highly educated citizenry."[2] Postmodern influences subtly deposited in the collective conscience of many communities comparable in size to my community are conscientiously celebrated in Corvallis, Oregon in every influential venue including university lecterns, theologically progressive pulpits, city council, public schools, and the local *Gazette Times*.

My beautiful Oregon community is among the four least churched communities, per-capita, in the United States (less than one in four people attend church).[3] My pastoral staff and I went to the neighborhoods in our community to ask people: "In your opinion, why don't people in Corvallis go to church?" We contacted approximately one thousand homes but we recorded only the responses from the un-churched. I chose the neighborhoods immediately surrounding Oregon State University.[4]

I went to the first home on the block, on the corner of 34th and Harrison, and introduced myself to an attractive, middle-aged lady with a pleasant, inviting smile. "In your opinion, why don't people in Corvallis go to church?" The lady's response was immediate, "I satisfy my spiritual life apart from any religious community . . . What I look for isn't in church; it's in humans." As

I thanked her and turned to walk down her steps, I could not help but wonder how dehumanized she must think the church has become!

I was preparing to walk back to the sidewalk at the second house, concluding no one was home, when finally a middle-aged, bath-robed, grumpy man with messed up hair, a scraggly beard and half-shut eyes came to the door. I briefly introduced myself and my intentions, "Hi, I'm the pastor of Kings Circle Assembly of God. I'm not here to try to convert you. If you would please indulge me, I would appreciate your response to just one question." The man starred at me for a moment as though he was trying to think of something to say, perhaps something like, "Go away!" After hearing my question, the man consented by saying, "Don't know, don't care."

The man at the next house seemed as though he had been waiting for me to show up on his doorstep; this was his opportunity to speak his mind. He cleared his throat, raised his bearded chin slightly, pushed out his bony chest, mentally locked and loaded and fired his reaction to my question: "Religion is meaningless, faith is meaningless, the church is without meaning." As he stood in his doorway with a very satisfied look on his face, he threw the door shut!

In the next block, a young man, appearing to be in his early thirties, answered the door. He was in a rush but nonetheless, obliged me: "Churches are too politically oriented. I can't relate to the church's perspective on gay-marriage." The lady next door also responded from a perceived perspective of the evangelical church's political alignment, "Republicans identify with the church; liberal Democrats don't." Two doors down the street a lady was entertaining her friends but graciously took a moment to respond to my question: "I'm a Democrat; your message isn't for me."

Although responses varied from home to home, they were painfully typical: "The church is seeking its own self-interest." "The hypocrisy we see." "Personal beliefs don't match institutional beliefs." "Corvallis is a detached community with no sense of need of the church." "Church is a place with no meaning." "I realized at a very young age that it wasn't a matter of belief but rather, it was a matter of church structure and control."

A POSTMODERN COMMUNITY'S PERSPECTIVE

Three outstanding perceptions of the church surfaced from our survey:

1. The church defines itself by who it excludes, particularly, Democrats, homosexuals, and people in general who are not like us.

2. The church's love is conditional: "If you will come to us and become like us, we will love you," is the perceived message to the host community.
3. The church places its needs above the needs of the community in its pursuit of political power. The postmodern "hermeneutic of suspicion" charges that the church's doctrinal certainty justifies its cultural imperialism and quest for political power while marginalizing those that are "outside."

The church's journey to Burning Man, that is to say the church's recovery of her vocation and the cultural transformation that follows, begins with hearing the culture's heart.

CULTURAL TRANSFORMATION IN THE TWENTY-FIRST CENTURY

There is no prescribed method, recipe, or formula for cultural transformation in the postmodern setting. Ministry is messy in the postmodern context—it is experimental; it is a journey marked by much trial and error therefore, it is not prescriptive. The application of the broad contours of Vital Christianity in this chapter is intended only to produce a poor reflection not a clear image of what the church is to be for the world. The means to effective ministry in any given postmodern setting (or for that matter, any world-view context) becomes increasingly clear as the church's journey leads her to join Jesus where he is and do what he is doing.[5]

BUILDING COMMUNITY

The church is the first-fruits of a new heaven and a new earth—the church is the first-fruits of the new world order. Stanley Hauerwas asserts:

> The work of Jesus was not a new set of ideals or principles for reforming or even revolutionizing society, but the establishment of a new community, a people that embodied forgiveness, sharing and self-sacrificing love in its rituals and discipline. In that sense, the visible church is not to be the bearer of Christ's message, but to be the message.[6]

The church is a paradigmatic society, "an eschatological sign of God's communal designs for the New Creation."[7] God's apocalyptic drama is played out on the margins; the presence and reality of the kingdom of God is revealed in the church's spiritual poverty—the church is a sacrament for the culture: she empties herself on the world's account as tangible evidence that God is renewing all things.

Believers have been reconciled to God through faith in Christ. And the church, "who are many" different people, different races, and different backgrounds must be reconciled one with another; there are not two tables but one.[8]

The Mosaic Church meets in a variety of locations in Los Angeles, California. Mosaic is a revelation of the power of the Cross through its symbolic expression of humanity's brokenness and fragmentation in the diverse make-up of its members. Mosaic is defined by who it includes: "Come to Mosaic, and discover how all the pieces can fit together!" Mosaic is a redeemed community of men and women representing "every corner of life."[9]

Mosaic is not alone; many churches in America are defining themselves by who they include in the likeness of Jesus' table-fellowship. These churches express divine grace and blessing in their host communities and throughout the earth. The church's journey towards the recovery of her vocation leads her to exchange wealth for spiritual poverty and relocate her ministry focus from the center to the margins.

CONTEXTUALIZING THE GOSPEL

In February, 2006, at the National Prayer Breakfast in Washington D.C., U2's lead singer, Bono, remarked:

> God is in the slums, in the cardboard boxes where the poor play house. God is in the silence of a mother who has infected her child with a virus that will end both their lives. God is in the cries heard under the rubble of war. God is in the debris of wasted opportunity and lives, and God is with us if we are with them.[10]

Beneath society's rubble is the Scum of the Earth, a church located in Denver, Colorado, and its daughter church, the Refuse of the World located in Colorado Springs, Colorado. The Scum of the Earth and the Refuse of the World take their names from Paul's self-description:

> To this very hour we go hungry and thirsty, we are in rags, we are brutally treated, we are homeless. We work hard with our own hands. When we are cursed, we bless; when we are persecuted, we endure it; when we are slandered, we answer kindly. Up to this moment we have become the scum of the earth, the refuse of the world. (1 Corinthians 4:11–13)

The Scum of the Earth and the Refuse of the World are examples of churches identifying with and connecting to the values of the host community; this is essential to the incarnation (contextualization) of the gospel. It is noteworthy that although The Refuse of the World's services are described as "pretty normal;" in the likeness of Jesus' table-fellowship, they stop in the middle of the service and have a meal together. "The fellowship involved in that is a holy thing and not something to be taken lightly."[11]

The complexity of twenty-first-century postmodern culture in the United States requires the transformation of society to be carried out from within the constituent parts of institutional structures not from without. Hill writes:

> In order to achieve a nationwide movement for community transformation that is institutionally based, key functionaries within each institution need to be active in having a shared vision of the overall objective, and to work with other committed Christians within that institution for the formation of a creative strategy of social change.[12]

The contextualization of the gospel is not about fixing an individual's situation, but about discipleship.[13] Discipleship involves preparing believers to discover through ministry participation ways to connect the life of the church and the reality of the kingdom of God to everyday life. To this end, the church needs to be *missional*—the church needs to go to people and move into their neighborhood instead of waiting for them to show up at church (James 2:5–17). Speaking of relocation, Bob Lupton stresses:

> [T]here is a growing consensus among committed urban practitioners that being a vested member of the community one is called to serve is an important key to effectiveness. What may seem to some like a very radical position is in fact proving to be the most practical approach to effective ministry in disadvantaged neighborhoods. Thus, relocation has become one of the "non-negotiables" of the Christian Community Development Association.[14]

The church is unprepared to understand the problems confronting the poor until their problems become the church's problems. Jesus was not accused of being "a glutton and a drunkard" (Matt. 11:9b NIV) because he was hanging out with ancient proto-types of Ward, June, Wally and Beaver Cleaver in suburbia Jerusalem—the poverty of Christ means Jesus became an outcast so that humanity no longer would be outcasts from the presence of God; the Incarnation required the Son of God's cosmic relocation!

Consequently, the effective contextualization of the gospel requires the church to be organic. The church acknowledges that the culture sets the agenda and therefore, adapts to the surroundings. The church needs to thoroughly understand the culture's images, metaphors, stories, and frameworks. Through this understanding, the church creatively enacts and retells the culture's stories in ways that communicate the gospel to people's deepest longings.[15] The church's story then becomes society's story and Christian symbols become society's sacred symbols.[16]

Martin Robertson and Dwight Smith penetrate to the heart of the contextualization of the gospel in twenty-first-century post-modernity: "Many churches in nations that are seeing a dramatic expansion of the kingdom are taking the natural and spontaneous passion of people and helping them to be much more intentional in their encounter with secular people."[17] Imago Dei, located in Portland, Oregon, is an example of what Robertson and Smith describe. Imago Dei's website rhetorically asks:

> What would it take for a neighborhood to be transformed by the gospel of Jesus Christ? As the people of God we eat, sleep, work in the garden, talk over the fence, patronize businesses, and take the kids to school in neighborhoods. That's pretty normal and could be temporal and fairly insignificant—unless you're traveling along on the missional journey of God. In that case it all takes on an eternal significance. The difference is determined by conscious awareness and cooperation with Jesus who is leading this journey. Where is he leading? Could it be into neighborhoods? Might he lead us to live in a particular neighborhood where we intentionally journey in mission for the sake of our neighbors?[18]

Imago Dei identifies "aching places" in the city of Portland and calls its members together to discuss, connect, and pray about some of them relocating to the aching places; redistributing resources for the common good in the aching places, and reconciling an aching neighborhood or business district to Christ's unconditional love. Imago Dei makes disciples of not-yet-Christians by being the presence of Christ for them.

"Proximity spaces" are creative means to be the presence of Christ. Proximity spaces are locations created for the purpose of Christians and not-yet-Christians coming together in meaningful dialogue. These spaces may be cafes, art galleries, design studios, sports clubs, or any place where casual yet meaningful interaction can take place among Christians and not-yet-Christians.

Among several stories about the missional success of proximity spaces told by Michael Frost and Alan Hirsch in *The Shape of Things to Come*, one particularly outstanding story is about the Subterranean Shoe Room, a retro-shoe store in San Francisco located on Valencia Street.

Brock Bingaman, a Southern Baptist church planter and evangelist, owns The Subterranean Shoe Room. Brock is a veteran church planter; however, San Francisco's cultural soil is unyielding to conventional purpose-driven churches like he was attempting to plant. Brock's efforts resulted in a failed spiritual crop forcing him to seek other employment for the sake of financial survival. Brock turned to something he loves, selling shoes.

Interestingly, Brock has loved shoes since childhood; he knows shoes and how to fit different styles of shoes with different personality types. Brock's standard approach to prospective cliental is: "Tell me about yourself and I'll tell you what shoes you need." People open up to Brock, they tell him much more about themselves than what kind of shoes they're looking for. After hearing their story, Brock presents them with a pair of shoes, perhaps a pair of pink Pumas or cherry-red Docs. The customers are delighted; rarely does Brock miss matching shoes and personalities.

The Southern Baptist evangelist laments about former methods of church planting: "As a church planter, I spent ninety percent of my time with Christians. . ." but "as a shoe salesman, I spend ninety percent of my time with non-Christians."[19] Brock has developed meaningful relationships with gay couples, Marxist professors, aging hippies, and bohemian artists, all types of people not normally vying with one another for the best seat in church. Brock has discovered a means by which to be the presence of Christ for a people group otherwise hostile to Christian faith.

God's apocalyptic agenda does not mean the end the world; God has reclaimed his creation through the bodily, physical resurrection of Jesus Christ from the dead. Creation is being renewed, restored, and recreated. Consequently, the church's proclamation of the Cross must be conflated with social and economic justice—the church must embrace Vital Christianity.

THE COMMON GOOD

If Christians fail to use their affluence to daily experience the life of those on the margins, they lose ethical currency vital for the transformation of culture; but when Christians do justice in behalf of the "least of these" (Matt. 25:31–46), unbelievers witness the Christian vision as believers contribute to the culture's common good and the healing of society's ills.

Educational systems, hospitals, orphanages, care for the poor, the homeless, widows, the dying, the mentally handicapped, and visiting the imprisoned have their origins in the gospel. Historically, the church has been the only entity on earth that exists for the benefit of all of its nonmembers.[20]

Throughout the history of the church, those who have been beneficiaries of the grace of God have been called to reveal Christ's poverty to their neighbors: the poor, the vulnerable, and the disenfranchised.[21] In a just society the perpetuation of poverty is not tolerated (Isa. 10:1–4; 58:3–12, Jer. 5:26–29; 22:13–19, Amos 2:6–7; 4:1–3; 5:10–15). Promoting the common good requires the church to share her many resources for the empowering of the poor and vulnerable in ways that enable them to sustain themselves.

Perkins asserts, "When we put the needs of the church ahead of the needs of those we are trying to reach with the gospel, we end up accommodating our heresy and hypocrisy. We need to empower the poor to reach the middle and upper classes of society."[22]

Perkins' Christian Community Development Association observes that isolation is the single greatest source for the perpetuation of poverty in major urban areas; the poor are isolated from the city's major service systems. When people with influence in the society relocate to the inner city, they are able to help connect the poor with the marketplace, the church, educational institutions and the political sphere.

The Christian Community Development Association's term for the empowering of the marginalized is "redistribution." Mary Nelson cites John Perkins' remarks in his *Beyond Charity* by way of the thinking behind redistribution:

> In the 1960s the motto of community development was "Give people a fish, and they'll eat for a day." In the 1970s it was "Teach people to fish, and they'll eat for a lifetime." In the 1990s the focus has turned to "Who owns the pond?" Perkins goes on to say, "The challenge for Christian community-based economic development is to enable the people of the community to start local enterprises that meet local needs and employ indigenous people."[23]

Redistribution for the common good is about empowering the marginalized to enact social and economic justice on their own behalf.

The Dream Center in Los Angeles is located on the margins; poverty, hopelessness, and violence are everywhere.[24] Concerning poverty, the Dream Center's website reports:

> The children are the most negatively affected. Nationally, 50% of Caucasian children and 80% of African-American children live in single-parent homes for at least part of their childhood. These children are five times more likely to live below the poverty line than children who live with both parents. In L.A., the rate of poverty among children is almost 50% higher than the poverty rate among the city's population as a whole. Most of these children will experience lives of gangs, drugs, crime and illicit sex.[25]

The Dream Center meets the enormous needs in its city by helping one person at a time. The Dream Center feeds, loves and helps the homeless: "We provide food for thousands of people who are homeless each week, as well as clothes, vocational training, our recovery program and shelter. We see hundreds of those we reach out to who are living on the streets, introduced to Jesus each week."[26] Through over 150 ministries, the Dream Center empowers the marginalized and restores hope to thousands of hurting people.[27]

Working for economic and social justice for the common good is not a solo effort. Co-belligerent partnerships are needed to end isolation for the poor and significantly contribute to the common good and transformation of culture.

CO-BELLIGERENCE

Co-belligerent relationships are critical for the funding of projects for the common good and consequent cultural transformation. Therefore, the local church must not allow fear of damage to their personal integrity to keep them from partnering with others committed to their goals, reforms and projects.[28] John Perkins and the Christian Community Development Association have effectively led community transformation in Mendenhall, Mississippi through co-belligerent partnerships.

Perkins has organized co-ops for poor African Americans. The Federation of Southern Co-ops is dedicated to the development of local resources and local income: "When we look at the poor getting poorer through the self-perpetuating cycle of ignorance, poor health and lack of opportunity, two truths are evident: (1) money must be made available to develop potential, and (2) the community itself must develop its potential to utilize and multiply economic resources."[29] Perkins teamed with the Farmers' Home Administration to help house the poor: "The overall goal of indigenous community vitality" brings economic empowerment to the poor. He has worked with tutorial programs and educational assistance particularly in helping the poor discover their own economic independence: "Federal handouts don't help. People themselves must be their own economic salvation."[30]

The People's Development Incorporated is a co-op dedicated to helping the poor with housing needs. Through this ministry, Perkins' strategy is to "seed" every neighborhood with two or three Christian families as a way to bring about community change. The People's Development Incorporated works for school integration. In the South, the last to integrate have been the churches.[31] The People's Development's contributions to economic and social justice include a general store, legal aid for the poor, a medical center for the poor housed in a formerly segregated medical building in downtown Mendenhall and staffed by a physician who is a committed part of Perkins' Voice of Calvary Ministries in Mendenhall; the Voice of Calvary Health Center in Jackson, Mississippi, a Christian Youth Center, and the first Bible Institute in Mendenhall and Jackson.

In 1982, Perkins and his wife, Vera Mae, returned to Southern California. His daughter, Elizabeth writes, "Of course, they chose to live on a street known for its cocaine dealers and stabbings."[32] Through partnerships in Los Angeles the Perkins established the Harambee Christian Family Center to meet the needs of children in Pasadena, California. The needs of children in Los Angeles are different from the needs of kids in rural Mississippi, gangs and drug dealers were picking up children at an early age. Many children were dropping out of school and getting into trouble with the law. Harambee started a tutoring program in the evening and many children responded.

Perkins began buying up the crack houses in the neighborhood and turning them into ministry centers. He started business training centers and eventually, he established a prep school. Perkins' strategy is to raise up in Christ some of the gifted kids who would subsequently change their neighborhoods. Perkins and his wife now live in Jackson, Mississippi where they established the Spencer Perkins Center for Reconciliation and Youth Development (named in honor of their late son).[33]

The kingdom of God is a present reality; the political agenda of the King calls the church to be the state's prophetic conscience.

APPLICATION: KINGDOM POLITICS AND CULTURAL TRANSFORMATION

Whereas strong consensus exists among Christians that the church ought to inform the state's conscience concerning social-ethical matters such as the plight of the vulnerable and poor, the sanctity of human life, racial reconciliation, the traditional family, the stewardship of the planet and the promotion of justice, freedom and peace, disagreement exists among Christian communions as to how the church ought to practically respond to her prophetic calling.

How should the Church enact the politics of the Kingdom?[34] Following a recovery of "Vital Christianity," I propose the practical application of kingdom politics through ecclesiastical *re-form,* cultural *re-connection* and participation with the eschatological Spirit in *re-creation.*

The practical application of Kingdom Politics by the church "to every corner of life" calls the church to *re-form* its mindset: the church needs to transform its present mindset from an external radical dualism to a worldview framed in an *inaugural eschatology,* the King has brought the kingdom; a *realized eschatology,* the present kingdom is the first-fruits of the kingdom to come, and a *restoration eschatology,* God is making all things new through the eschatological Spirit. A biblical world and life view, cast in the unifying themes of Jesus' table-fellowship, invokes personal realization of the presence of the kingdom *everywhere*, throughout the earth.

A revival of Vital Christianity in the Church conflates social and economic justice—*reconnecting* with culture through the *contextualization* (incarnation) of the gospel; and the promotion of the *common good* of culture, often through *co-belligerent* relationships; and the proclamation of the cross and resurrection of Jesus Christ resulting in *new creation*, first among humanity and ultimately, throughout all of God's creation—the church is called to participate in the divine plan of the Holy Spirit's *re-creation* of God's world.

A POLITICS OF *RE-FORM*

The present kingdom is the first-fruits of the future kingdom; the future kingdom will deliver the cosmos from sin and death.[35] Churchill observed that democracy is the worst form of government *except* for all the other forms tried from time to time.[36] The problem of evil is not resolved through democracy, but through allegiance to the King of the kingdom of God. From God's self-surrender manifest in Christ's poverty, Christians derive an ethic of surrender universally applicable to all of human life; surrender to the Lordship of Christ transcends all earthly political commitments.

President James Madison, like Wilberforce, was a rare statesman. Madison's insightful link between faith, civil society, and republican government laid the foundation for a secular democracy that nonetheless depended on the integral role of religious faith and the church. Indeed, government *ought* to be secular, but this is why the state needs a transcendent moral/ethical referent—a prophetic conscience (Romans 13:1–5). Martin Luther King Jr. asserted, "[The] church must be reminded that it is not the master or the servant of the state, but rather the conscience of the state. It must be the guide and the critic of the state, and never its tool."[37]

However, the prophetic conscience of the state, the evangelical church, has become a tool of right-wing partisan politics; and consequently, the evangelical church has alienated the major political party on the left and millions of its constituents.

The evangelical church is contributing to the political and social polarization in the nation instead of acting as peacemaker. The church's responsibility is to be for the political sphere (and culture) what it cannot be for itself—the church is not to hold those on the left in contempt, neither is it to be co-dependent on those on the right, but rather it is to provide moral/ethical guidance for the whole of the political sphere.

For the church to recover her divinely ordained role as the state's prophetic conscience she must assume an independent witness—the evangelical church must resign its role as a tool of the Republican Party and offer an olive branch to the Democratic Party and its constituency. Political unity in America ought to be an all-consuming priority for the church. Indeed, a unified nation is more likely to reverse and/or write into law the great social-ethical concerns of the church than is a divided nation.

The party of William Jennings Bryan and Franklin D. Roosevelt has had a long tradition of social justice. The marginalized, the weak, the infirmed, and the most vulnerable have been at the heart of the Democratic agenda. The evangelical church must seek common ground with the Democratic Party and commit to working with those on the left side of the aisle—the church's reconciliation with the Democratic Party may serve to significantly advance the church's cause for social and economic justice.[38]

God's calling of the church to be the prophetic conscience for the state and culture begins with the church's recognition of the need for change in the culture beyond the passage of mere legislation; the entire political moral/ethical context in which politicians and society function must be reformed.

Further, the Christian worldview must encompass both domestic and foreign policy. Although Christians differ on many issues, they are consistently together concerning human dignity and the protection and welfare of the most vulnerable. The Evangelical Church has been much too willing to compromise principle and conviction for access to the center of [earthly] power. The church must surrender her pursuit of political power in favor of solidarity with the weak, the exploited, and the disenfranchised in America and worldwide. The church needs to hear God's prophet with hearts inclined towards righteousness and obedient determination to "do justice, love kindness, and walk humbly with your God" (Micah 6:8).

A POLITICS OF *RE-CONNECTION*

In speaking of the triune God's dissimilarity with humans, Lewis contends, "That God is God, and different from us, is nowhere plainer than in human beings' demonstrable unwillingness to enter into solidarity and oneness with each other, and especially with those perceived to be different from themselves."[39]

According to Jim Wallis:

The greatest moral question in American politics today is, "What is our prosperity for? Will it serve as an excuse to forget those left behind? Or will it include those who have fallen through the cracks in our society, including almost thirteen million children?" The biblical prophets say that a society's integrity is judged, not by its wealth and power, but by how it treats its most vulnerable members.[40]

In the face of great fear, exploitation, and injustice, Jesus' incarnation, death, and resurrection have become the symbols of God's counter-ideological opposition to the totalizing violence of the majority. The Creator of all humanity, himself a marginalized Jew, embraced "marginality and pain, on behalf of *both* the margins and the center."[41] The blood of the Cross united Jew and Gentile, slave and free, those on the margins and those at the center.[42]

The kingdom of God has come and the earth is "full of the knowledge of the Lord as the waters cover the sea": a politics of *re-connection* calls a Spirit-empowered church to implement the reality of the present kingdom and enact—for the *common good*—the reconciling power of the Gospel. This means *co-belligerence* with other people and groups at home and abroad: "It's as simple as identifying extraordinary people and getting them the resources they need to do what they need to do. We can't do it. The key to all kinds of development is just finding local partners, principled people who want to make a difference in their own country."[43]

A POLITICS OF *RE-CREATION*

The politics of *re-creation* conflates social justice and the proclamation of the Gospel—a politics of *re-creation* is a revival of Wilberforce's Vital Christianity. A politics of *re-creation* means God's love always triumphs over evil, trust and understanding subvert suspicion and hostility, and the promotion of peace brings healing to fractured communities. "Only in a more just world will humanity begin to learn how much more rewardingly postures and practices of peace and trust may prosper beyond the impressive but abortive efficaciousness of force."[44]

The Resurrection points to new creation rather than creation's apocalyptic doom—the risen Christ reigns over every sphere of life. Consequently, a realized eschatology is paradigmatic for the politics of *re-creation*—in Christ, the future has been brought into the present; continuity exists between our present corruptible life and our future incorruptible life and this brings meaning to every part of human life.

A politics of *re-creation* provides impetus for Christians to be involved in politics at every level, from city council to the President of the United States. It urges participation with others in the political process to resist evil and promote peace and justice analogous to God's future, ultimate coming kingdom.

The message of Easter commissions the church to call for the "transformation of politics."[45] Fundamentally, goodness needs to be considered virtuous in our culture including in the political sphere. Without a seismic shift in political vision in the United States, biblical efforts to address great social-ethical issues are likely to fail. A politics of *re-creation* brings "God's compassion to the oppressed as well as opposes the oppressors"[46]

Wilberforce's political philosophy resurfaces at this point: a politics of *re-creation* involves a conscientious application of the "Golden Rule": Christian stewardship, respect for the rights of others, advancement of others' views, and promotion of the happiness of others. A politics of *re-creation* is a sacred duty for all people, especially Christians.

Politics, therefore, ought to be grounded in the moral consensus of the culture; the culture should shape politics rather than the other way around. Christianity ought to shape the culture, rather than the other way around; therefore, Christians seeking to shape public policy must extensively research social, historical, jurisprudential, and political trends.

Wilberforce and the Clapham Sect's political philosophy was grassroots. A politics of *re-creation* wisely adopts the Clapham strategy of extensive field research among the general populace for the purpose of discovering ways and means of relating to and meeting society's deepest longings.

Solidarity with the "least of these" (Matt. 25:31–46) is solidarity with Christ's impoverishment. "Nurtured through this reconciliation shall be a surplus in God's final kingdom of peace and justice over violence and unrighteousness—concrete, visible signs of which can and must be fashioned within our social ordering today."[47] Just as the British conscience was moved by the Clapham Group's acts of unconditional love, the conscience of America would be moved by the church's unselfishness and compassion for those on the margins and the *common good* of culture.

A groundswell of public support would force the hand of Congress to pass the Church's moral-ethical reforms.[48] Members of the judicial, legislative, and executive branches of the United States government would be accountable to the public—the American people, for their immorality and corruption.

CONCLUSION: WATER BAPTISM AND THE CHURCH'S VOCATION

The sacred ordinance of Water Baptism is a symbol of the church's vocation to be for the world what it cannot be for itself. Water Baptism is "post-individualistic"[49]—Water Baptism reminds the church it is called to unveil a new humanity to the world.

Through Christ's sufferings and afflictions, humanity belongs to him (Rom. 14:7–8), and by belonging to Christ, humanity belongs to one another. The new covenant community transcends both modernity and post-modernity and "their equally inhuman agendas of assimilation and fragmentation."[50]

Water Baptism is performed in the name of the Father, the Son and the Holy Spirit—"these words say absolutely nothing new even while they compress all of salvation history into three personal names."[51] Water Baptism reminds the church of Christ's restoration eschatology and consequently, the need to *reconnect* with and participate with the Spirit in the *recreation* of culture through the incarnation and proclamation of the gospel.

Water Baptism informs the church to initiate her recovery mission from the starting point of what she is through faith in Christ. Baptism ushers in a new age and a new humanity; the old creation was buried with Christ in death and through Christ's resurrection, the new creation has begun: "The new creation is not simply regenerated individuals but the renewal of all things, in which believers participate by new birth."[52]

The eschatological work of the Spirit is the renewing of all things and as the first-fruits of new creation, the *re-forming* church, organic by nature, is always reforming (*Semper Reformanda*), always adapting to its changing cultural context, and always participating with the Spirit in the *re-creating* of God's creation—the simplicity and beauty of the sacraments, the wash and the meal, remind the church of her calling to be a sacrament for the world. The church's application of Kingdom Politics by means of a politics of *re-form,* a politics of *re-connection* and a politics of *re-creation* is illustrated in figure 4.1.

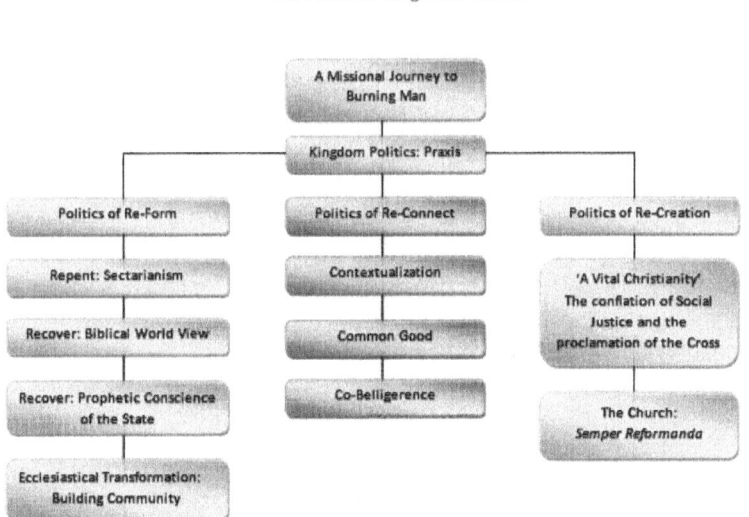

Figure 4.1.

NOTES

1. Since writing this book, the author and his wife have relocated to Minneapolis, Minnesota.

2. Steve Ames, "Community Visioning: Planning for the Future in Oregon's Local Communities," *Contrast and Transition*, 1997.

3. Patricia O'Connell Killen and Mark Silk, eds. *Religion and Public Life in the Pacific Northwest* (Toronto, Canada: Roman and Littlefield, 2004), 23.

4. In keeping with the university's postmodern identity, the school has dropped "university" from its name.

5. The means the application of Kingdom Politics, the focus of Chapter 5.
Restoring At-Risk Communities (Grand Rapids, MI: Baker, 1995), edited by John Perkins is a source of my inspiration for this chapter. Perkins and other authors associated with his organization, Christian Community Development Association, discuss his three "Rs" for cultural transformation: relocation, reconciliation and redistribution. By "relocation," Perkins is referring to the non-negotiable need to live within the particular community that you are attempting to bring transformation; by "reconciliation" Perkins refers to an integrated Christian community that reflects God's willingness to reconcile humanity to himself and by "redistribution" Perkins is speaking of people reconciled to God and one another sharing whatever resources they have to work together for the common good of the community. The principles bound up in the three "Rs" are applicable in each unique postmodern setting. The principles inherent in Perkins' three "Rs" will surface in this chapter.

6. Jason Byassee, "Emerging Model: A Visit to Jacob's Well," *The Christian Century*, September, 2006, 1–6.

7. Richard Mouw and John H. Yoder, "Evangelical Ethics and the Anabaptist-Reformed Dialogue," in *Toward An Evangelical Public Policy*, eds. Ronald J. Sider and Diane Knippers (Grand Rapids, MI: Baker, 2005), 132. According to reformed theologian Michael Horton, "Evangelical Christians are as likely to embrace lifestyles every bit as hedonistic, materialistic, self-centered, and sexually immoral as the world in general." The Church must discover compassionate and self-giving ways to recover her image and credibility in society.

8. Divisiveness in the Body of Christ is a sign to the host community that the blood of Christ no longer reconciles sinful humanity to God; therefore, those who cause division must be removed from the church.

9. Mosaic, "Home," Mosaic, http://www.mosaic.org., (11–15–07).

10. Bono, "54th Annual National Prayer Breakfast Speech," February 2, 2006, *The Worshipper*, Summer 2006, 22.

11. The Refuse of the World, "Home," http://www.therefuse.net/about.html, (11–15–07).

12. Hill, The Wilberforce Connection, 361.

13. Haddon Robinson comments on the contemporary church's exchanging discipleship for consumerism: "Too often now when people join a church, they do so as consumers. If they like the product, they stay. If they do not, they leave. They can no more imagine a church disciplining them than they could a store that sells goods

disciplining them. It is not the place of the seller to discipline the consumer. In our churches we have a consumer mentality," quoted in Ronald Sider, *The Scandal of the Evangelical Mind*, 115.

14. Bod Lupton, "Relocation, Living in the Community," in *Restoring At-Risk Communities*, ed. John M. Perkins (Grand Rapids, MI: Baker, 1995), 75–76. Perkins' term, "relocation" is synonymous with "contextualizing" the gospel.

15. This thought is developed in Chapter 5, "Apologetics in the Postmodern Setting: Jesus at the Java Shop."

16. In many instances, postmodernists' attraction to mystery and their openness to spiritual experiences draw them to Christian symbols, particularly those associated with the Eucharist: incense, holy water, candles, and the host itself.

17. Martin Robinson and Dwight Smith, *Invading Secular Space* (Oxford, UK: Monarch, 2003), 187.

18. Imago Dei Community: http://www.imagodeicommunity.com (11–15–07).

19. Michael Frost and Alan Hirsch, *The Shape of Things to Come* (Peabody, MA: Hendrickson, 2003), 23–24.

20. Archbishop William Temple is cited for this observation in *Towards an Evangelical Public Policy*, 232.

21. Resources and agencies willing to work with the church for the common good abound in American communities. Correctional systems openly welcome Christian ministry into the prison system. State and county government is willing to work alongside the church to provide care for AIDS/HIV victims. Drug and alcohol treatment agencies and centers are responsive to the church's offer to come alongside of them. CASA, Court Appointed Special Advocates, places and supervises children in foster homes. CASA is open to Christians and churches helping in the placement and supervision process.

22. John Perkins was the keynote speaker for the New Wine, New Wineskins' Spring Conference, April 10–14, 2007 in Portland, Oregon. The Conference was hosted by the Institute for the Theology of Culture, Portland, Oregon. The theme of the conference was: "For the Least of These." Although Perkins did not graduate from elementary school, he holds nine honorary doctorates. Perkins has courageously fought for racial and social equality in the South as part of his proclamation of the gospel. Perkins' tireless work for racial reconciliation in America has included the role of counselor for several US Presidents to include Presidents Clinton and Bush.

23. Mary Nelson, "Redistribution, Empowering the Community," *Restoring At-Risk Communities*, 139–40.

24. Homelessness is staggering in L.A.; some 80,000 people sleep on the city's sidewalks every night; an estimated 60–80 % of the homeless struggle with mental or emotional illnesses. Most of the homeless have no food for several days out of any given week. One in six families in L.A. live below the poverty line. The average family income among the poor has declined by 24% since 1967. Community resources are limited and most of the city's shelters have six-month waiting lists. See, The Dream Center, "Home," The Dream Center, http://www.dreamcenter.org/the_need.php (11–15–07).

25. Ibid.

26. Ibid.

27. In the first four years of the Dream Center's outreach, prostitution, and gang violence decreased by 73 percent, homicides dropped by 28 percent, and rapes were down by 53 percent. The mayor and city council have praised the contributions to the common good by the L.A. Dream Center. President George W. Bush has acknowledged the L.A. Dream Center as a "model for faith-based organizations." Ibid. The Dream Center's website reports that 130 Dream Centers are now located throughout the United States and internationally, Canada, Sweden, and Australia have Dream Centers.

28. See Chapter 3, for a definition and historical context for co-belligerent relationships.

29. John Perkins, New Wine Spring Conference: "For the Least of These," April 10–14, 2007, Portland, Oregon.

30. Ibid.

31. Ibid.

32. Elizabeth Perkins, *Let Justice Roll Down*, 82.

33. Inspired by Wilberforce's co-belligerent efforts, our church in Corvallis, Oregon constructed an assisted living center. West Hills Assisted Living Community is the result of a partnership with a corporation in a nearby city. The board made plans to further develop our "community of care" by partnering with another corporation from Washington to build a memory care center and a retirement facility. This construction is planned to take place before the church will construct a new church building. The Medicaid assisted living facility is a need in the community and the church has showed Corvallis, Oregon they desire to place them before themselves. Income from these facilities would make available financing for missional ministry to the poor and vulnerable in the community.

34. Allan Lewis answers this question by means of introducing a three-fold approach to kingdom politics for the church corporate and individual Christians. According Lewis, a "politics of surrender" involves, "the pain of giving away, of giving up, of letting go;" a "politics of similarity" is "designed to encourage authorities and governments to foster community understanding and strengthen bonds of mutual interest and support between parties estranged and reciprocally fearful and suspicious," and a "politics of superfluity" means love always triumphs over evil, trust and understanding subvert suspicion and hostility, and the promotion of peace brings healing to fractured communities. My proposal is an adaptation of Lewis' thought; Alan E. Lewis, *Between Cross & Resurrection, A Theology of Holy Saturday* (Grand Rapids, MI: Eerdmans, 2001), 308–328.

35. Lewis' description of a politics of surrender fits well here in our discussion: This is to say that though there is an Easter victory, a fecundity of life in the midst of death, which shall redeem and transform history, the only way to that future and to its temporal anticipations here and now passes through barrenness and negativity. God can no more come to the divine tomorrow of consummation and fulfillment than we can to ours, without first embracing suffering, defeat, and death. More specifically, our non-optimistic hopes of participating in history's future of justice, peace, and freedom cannot be separated from the imperative upon us, as upon the God of

history's own self, to countenance the varieties and costs of *surrender*: the pain of giving away, of giving up, of letting go, Ibid.

36. Please do not miss my point; this statement appears radical only to those who confuse democracy with kingdom politics. The rest of my statement clarifies my point. Additionally, Christians hold dual-citizenship: we are citizens of the kingdom of God and, in my case and perhaps the majority of my readers, the United States of America.

37. Martin Luther King Jr., *Strength To Love* (New York: Harper and Row, 1963). Cf. Romans 13:1–7; 1Peter 2:13–17. God has ordained the church and the state as independent of one another and each has distinct callings in their service to Him.

38. The church must take the lead, for "redistribution" is the church's calling, not the government's calling. When the government attempts to do what the church is called to do the result is the paralyzing of the economy through socialism or worse, communism; when the church attempts to do what government is called to do, the result is an oppressive theocracy.

39. Ibid., 312.

40. Wallis, God's Politics, 236.

41. J. Richard Middleton and Brian J. Walsh, "Facing the Postmodern Scalpel, Can the Christian Faith Withstand Deconstruction?" in *Christian Apologetics in the Postmodern World*, eds. J. Richard Middleton and Brian J. Walsh (Downers Grove, IL: Inter-Varsity Press, 1995), 153.

42. Cf. Galatians 3:28; Ephesians 2:1ff; Romans 5:11; 1 Corinthians 1:30; Colossians 1:22.

43. Collin Hansen, "How Then Shall We Politick?" *Christianity Today,* August 2006, 38–41.

44. ibid., 323.

45. Ibid., 315.

46. Charles Colson, forward to *A Practical View of Christianity* by William Wilberforce, xii.

47. Ibid., 324.

48. See *Toward An Evangelical Public Policy* for detailed proposals of moral-ethical reforms that ought to be championed by the church.

49. The term, "post-individualistic" is used by Andy Crouch, "Life After Postmodernity," 14.

50. Ibid., 82.

51. Andy Crouch, 85.

52. Ibid., 81.

Chapter Five

'Jesus at the Java Stop': A Grassroots Application of Kingdom Politics

"Got faith?" queries *The Barometer's* humor columnist,

"I don't. I WISH I did. But I don't. Creation sounds so much better than my current theory that life spontaneously spawned from the waste of a giant star fart.

Jesus loves me, this I know. For the Bible tells me so. But when the oceans turn red and the last trumpet sounds, Jesus will be standing at the right hand of the Father with sparks in His pretty blue eyes, and this is what He'll say: "Go to hell, David"—All because I could not find faith in a faithless world. Can you feel the love?

The stormy beginning of this hump-week has put me in a pensive mood. Divine tears seemed to flow from the heavens in torrents, mixing with the blazing leaves in a Picasso-dream of liquid fire on a watercolor campus. Nature's blushing hues jump out of the gray with murderous beauty. It's a wonder that I doubt the existence of a Master Painter.

You need God in your life. How many times have you heard that? Without a personal relationship with the invisible silent One, you can . . . kiss your eternity goodbye. Start planning your eternal vacation to Hades, my fellow sinners. There'll be lots of us making hotel reservations and such, so you better jump on it.

Unfortunately for us, God doesn't exist in our cursed postmodern world. I wish He did. But He doesn't. If I see Jesus sippin' a cappuccino at the Java Stop tomorrow, I might be tempted to change my mind.

I was born a Christian. I know the 411 on God, yo. I got suckers and stars in Sunday school. Old folks smiled in approval every time I screamed "Hallelujah." My dad had a six-inch scraggly beard and made me say grace at the dinner table. You get the picture.

I escaped to college, the cock crowed thrice, and the world went on, better than ever. It's the same backslidden, guilt-ridden story that most of you have swept under the carpet, or drowned in a bottle, so I won't burden you with mine.

I can't take anymore rhetoric; I want to see the stories fulfilled—A leap of faith; an act of unmistakable power. Speech is nothing more than broken air. . . . I want to see some action!

If God exists, I pray that He'll strike me down where I sit. I give Him full leave to do so. I relinquish my right to His hands-off free will BS. Blasphemous, I know. But hey, I'm still writing. I'm still waiting; Yea for me; Nay for God.

Doctrine is nothing more than disguised fascism. It's for the birds to crap on. I can blow holes in it the size of pumpkins.

I envy all you who have faith, but I don't want your religion. Hurling doctrine from the street corners is not going to convince this faithless, surface-infatuated TV generation. We need to see the power of that Holy Spirit dude Christians say exists, not the biting irony of a frustrated preacher man.

It may seem that I and the rest of my faithless brethren attack Christianity excessively. Maybe it's because we're tired of a religion that has tried unsuccessfully for 2,000 years to recapture and exploit the power of a mysterious carpenter from Nazareth."[1]

The church in America *does not* lack knowledge, money, or access to power—we *lack* compassion. The prophet Jeremiah, and our Lord Jesus Christ, looked upon Jerusalem through tears. The American church must look upon her culture—from the White House to the halls of Congress, to the business district in Manhattan, to our university campuses, to the homosexual community in West Hollywood and to the "Strip" in Las Vegas through tears.

Through tears, this chapter exhorts the church to:

1. Read the signs;
2. And join Jesus at the Java Stop;
3. And compassionately apply Kingdom Politics for the transformation of your particular cultural context.

SEMIOTICS: READING THE SIGNS

In the opening scene of *The Fellowship of the Ring* the elf queen, Galadriel observes, "The world is changing. I see it in the water. I feel it in the earth. I smell it in the air."[2] Former assumptions about reality; and even the inherent meaning of language, formerly thought to be indispensable for the purpose of making sense of the world, have radically changed.

Jacques Derrida's axiom, "All the world's a text," suggests our semiotic duty to read the signs and see "the world is changing," to "see it in the water;" to "feel it in the earth," and even "smell it in the air."[3]

Sign-posts marking the church's journey to "Burning Man" include:

1. Postmodernism's rejection of meta-narratives; the postmodern "hermeneutic of suspicion" charges that all claims to *the* truth serve to legitimate the power structures of the majority while justifying the marginalizing of those perceived to be "outside;" "*Doctrine is nothing more than disguised fascism.*"[4]
2. A pluralistic ideology promoting a radical skepticism; the "informed" do not make truth-claims; "*hurling doctrine from the street corners is not going to convince this faithless, surface-infatuated TV generation.*"
3. The deconstructed world of postmodernism makes an author's identity or intention irrelevant where the interpretation of a text is concerned; there is no meaning to be found in the text—language is arbitrary and capricious and does not correspond to any overarching absolute linguistic laws: "*Speech is nothing more than broken air.*"

How should the church respond to the postmodern culture? Should the church start by constructing a new postmodern identity or by deconstructing an old modern one? A postmodern façade or attempting to be anything but modern is not the solution; the postmodern world wants "*to see some action!*"

COMMON GROUND

How can the church discover common ground—a normative understanding of how we *know*—with the postmodern culture? Knowledge achieving the status of a norm requires the resolve of a two-sided question: "who decides what knowledge is, and who knows what needs to be decided?"[5] Wittgenstein's resolve is to differentiate the modes of language in terms of "language games."[6] The term "language games" means that the properties of the various language categories are defined and properly used according to particular rules, "in exactly the same way as the game of chess is defined by a set of rules determining the properties of each of the pieces, in other words, the proper way to move them."[7]

Lyotard's observations regarding the "rules" to be used in making proper linguistic moves, extends Christian understanding for the development of an effective apologetic in the postmodern context:

> The first is that their rules do not carry within themselves their own legitimation, but are the object of a contract, explicit or not, between players (which is not to say that the players invent the rules). The second is that if there are no rules, there is no game, that even an infinitesimal modification of one rule alters the

nature of the game, that a "move" or utterance that does not satisfy the rules does not belong to the game they define. The third remark is suggested by what has just been said: every utterance should be thought of as a "move" in a game.[8]

In the postmodern context, "narratives allow the society in which they are told, on the one hand, to define its criteria of competence and, on the other, to evaluate according to those criteria what is performed or can be performed within it."[9] In other words, setting forth the gospel in narrative form—telling the story of the gospel (as opposed to propositional assertions) is a "proper way to move" the different "pieces" (truth-claims) of the gospel in the postmodern setting.

Narratives provide the effective mode for the gospel to become normative in the hearing of a postmodern community, and "proper moves" in the context of the gospel narrative will give rise to its universal implications.[10] The practical application of a narrative apologetic follows.

'JESUS AT THE JAVA STOP'

Chapter 1, "Following Jesus to Burning Man," illustrates the practical application of apologetics as constructed narratives. First, a narrative apologetic is contextual. To reach Burners, believers must follow Jesus to Burning Man and become like Burners (1 Cor. 9:22)—Christians are called to be the presence of Christ in every corner of *"our cursed postmodern world."*

Jesus is waiting for the local church to join him in the culture; Christ is not waiting for the culture to join him at church. The local "Java Stop" is a symbol of cultural activity and community—indeed, for some of us, coffee is almost as essential as air to breath: "Life is hard enough with coffee. What would life be without coffee?"[11]

Joining Jesus at the Java Stop is the spiritual equivalent of re-enacting Jesus' table-fellowship within the culture; the church is called to join Jesus wherever he is and be a sacrament for the world. In other words, *"If I see Jesus sippin' a cappuccino at the Java Stop tomorrow, I might be tempted to change my mind."*

Second, a narrative apologetic is dialogical. It is not designed to answer a wide range of theoretical questions but rather it is an exchange of stories, a sharing of experiences that arise from the particular situation. "Why are you here? Why did you come to Burning Man, Mick?" are questions critical for the setting of the rules of the dialogue and making the right moves for the delivery of a narrative apologetic. In the most practical terms, the proper delivery of a narrative apologetic requires the believer to exchange the role of teacher (the modernist paradigm), for facilitator (the postmodern paradigm).

Third, the Christian's story is subversive. When "signs of exile" are discerned in the expressions of the not-yet-Christian's heart, they must be concretely addressed from the circumstances of the Christian's life with a better story, the gospel story (the person or community will inform the believer or the church of the right moves if we are listening).

Mick came to Burning Man seeking a transcendent experience. My calling was to patiently allow him to define the rules for our dialogue and listen to his heart. Then I carefully related his longings to my defense of the gospel and the transcendent experience Christ could give him that would meaningfully fill every part of his life—now and forever.

Postmodernists are pragmatists, *"We need to see the power of that Holy Spirit dude Christians say exist."* The fourth element in the postmodern apologetic calls for the new covenant community to symbolically enact the restoration eschatology of Jesus in the power of the Spirit: *"I want to see the stories fulfilled"*—the whole gospel meets the needs of the whole person.

The proclamation of the gospel must be conflated with visible signs of compassion; the gospel includes social and economic justice for the marginalized, "those perceived to be outside"—"a Vital Christianity" is called for![12] The church's compassion for those "perceived to be 'outside'" suspends the postmodern hermeneutic of suspicion and brings credibility to the gospel for both those on the margins and at the center; and the world witnesses the Spirit empowered church, *"recapture and exploit the power of a mysterious carpenter from Nazareth."*

Every time the postmodernist returns—as Mick returned—to say, "We want to hear you again on this subject" (Acts 17:32) the universal implications of the gospel are increasingly heard and, hearing calls for confession: "Jesus is Lord," and *"a leap of faith; an act of unmistakable power*—Resurrection power! (Rom. 10:9). Believers must always be prepared to both be the story and *tell* the story (1 Peter 3:15)—"Wherever you go, preach the gospel, and when necessary, use words" (St. Francis).

A GRASSROOTS APPLICATION OF KINGDOM POLITICS

How can you, as a pastor (or church leader) facilitate a meeting with your church leadership to discuss, in practical terms, "how is our church going to go about *doing* all of this"?

The following is a proposed grassroots application of Kingdom Politics: phase 1: a politics of *re-form;* phase 2: a politics of *re-connection* and phase 3: a politics of *re-creation*. My proposal answers:

1. Approximately how long is each phase?
2. What type of questions should church leadership ask themselves in each phase?
3. What are some resources that will help our church leadership effectively apply a politics of *re-form*, a politics of *re-connection* and a politics of *re-creation* for the transformation of our particular cultural context?

DOING GRASSROOTS CULTURAL TRANSFORMATION

The church's application of kingdom politics—a politics of *re-form*, a politics of *reconnection* and a politics of *re-creation* "to every corner of life" provides context for the transformation of the church's mindset from an external radical dualism to the realization of the presence of the kingdom *everywhere*, throughout the earth. The church's living out of Vital Christianity includes the conflation of social justice—the church's transforming *re-connection* with culture and the proclamation of the Gospel—the church's participation with the Spirit in *re-creation*.

Development and the anticipated duration of each phase of the practical application of Kingdom Politics is set-forth below (also, resources critical to each phase are suggested for the consultation of church leadership).

A Missional Journey: Phase 1: *Re-Form*: Minimum Time: 1–2 years

The subversion and recreation of the church's conscience in the image of modernity produced "Christendom." Modernity (the Enlightenment's offspring) is the primary influence behind the church's privatization of the Christian faith—the Western Church (the model of the church known as Christendom) is charged with the responsibility of caring for the inner, private, religious life of people. And consequently, Christendom occupies an inner, private space, removed from the public sphere—the world of politics, science, business, education and the arts. The church is exiled from the public (secular) sphere to the private sphere of the individual in need of its religious goods.

The private (sectarian) sphere of the church sees the public (secular) sphere as "them"—an impasse exists in the mind of the Christian between the public sphere *outside* of the church and the private sphere *inside* the church.

Remarkably, the people we choose to separate ourselves from are the opposite of those whom Christ distinguished himself from—Christ is more identified with the riff-raff; the ancient "burners" than he is with the religious center and politically powerful.

A politics of *Re-Form* begins with a change of mindset in the church followed by a fundamental question: how far removed from the type of ministry worthy of the charge, "a glutton and a drunkard," is your church? How can you prepare your church to read the signs and realize that the "world is changing"; to "see it in the water"; to "feel it in the earth" and "smell it in the air"?

Building a *missional* community calls for the transformation of the church from a church-centered thinking *institution* to a culturally marginal thinking *organism*. The transforming of the otherwise slanderous charge, "a glutton and a drunkard" into a calling; a renewal of compassion for the marginalized, and the empowerment of the church to be for the culture what it cannot be for itself is the first phase of the church's journey.

Phase one is the practical employment of a *politics of re-form*: the transformation of the church to a biblical world view results in the body of Christ's realization of her need to repent of her external radical dualistic posture towards culture (sectarianism) and join Jesus on the margins—the wash and meal are symbols of the church's vocation to be for the world what it cannot be for itself (re: Chapters 2 and 4). Timely questions to ask at this phase of the church's journey follow:

Missional Leadership Must Discover

- Does our church leadership discern the need to *re-form*?
- Where is our church in its spiritual journey?
- What is our understanding of a Christian World-View?
- How can we effectively introduce the need for our church to *re-form*?
- How can we create environments to facilitate dialogue about the Christian world-view? How can we inspire our church to see that the "world is changing"; to "see it in the water"; to "feel it in the earth" and "smell it in the air"?

This phase (like the other two phases) requires enduring patience on the part of leadership. Leadership (inclusive of the pastoral staff and lay-leadership) must *re-form*—transform its thinking—before it is prepared to call the church to *re-form*.

Leadership ought to seek training, models and mentors before it approaches the larger congregation with the need to *re-form*. Several outstanding websites are listed in Appendix 2 of this book for the purpose of providing consultation for your church's leadership. Among the most valuable sources at this stage are:

Resources for Phase 1

- Charles Colson & Nancy Pearcey, *How Now Shall We Live?* (Wheaton, Ill.: Tyndale Publishers, 1999) is an excellent, and exhaustive, development of

the Christian World-View in the postmodern context. (See also, Chapter 2 and Appendix 1).
- Mission-Shaped Church Survey: http://www.allelon.net/missional_resources/church_survey.cfm

    This survey serves to help your church discover the missional life as well as the obstacles that stand between your church and missional ministry. The results of your survey are compiled into a comprehensive report that will give your leadership a vivid picture of where your church is in its spiritual journey and recommended actions for missional preparedness. An experienced coach is available for your church leadership to help you interpret and apply the results of the survey. (An example survey is available on the Allelon website).
- www.leonardsweet.com – This is the web site of my mentor; this site is rich in wisdom and insight in how to shape a congregation in the Christian world-view; how to read the signs and discern the longings of culture.
- www.redeemer.com – This is Redeemer Presbyterian and Tim Keller's web site. Tim Keller provides examples of sermons prepared in a narrative mode to address the postmodern world; articles that offer wise insight into our culture and an example, through Redeemer Presbyterian, of how the church can be for the world what it cannot be for itself!

If you begin the *re-form* phase with approximately 25% of your church (the influencers and those ready to respond) by the close of this phase and the beginning of the next, you will probably lose approximately 10–20% of the original 25%. This is because (1) most people are not given to change, they rather resist it and (2) as missional awareness sets in, so does discontentment with the church's refocusing from church-centered ministry to culture-centered ministry (particularly ministry among the marginalized).

Although you will lose some of your lay-leadership at the close of this first phase, it is important to initially include the influencers in your church because "buy-in" on their part will inspire the congregation. The remaining leadership will be well prepared to help pastoral leadership bring the rest of the church into the missional life.[13]

Bringing the church into the missional life initiates phase 2—*Re-Connect*.

A Missional Journey: Phase 2: *Re-Connect*:
Minimum Time: 1 Year

This phase requires creativity and imagination on the part of church leadership. During this phase, church leadership is committed to the retelling of the church's story cast in the non-dualistic frame of the second chapter's portrait of "A Glutton and A Drunkard"!

Phase 2 involves the practical application of a *politics of re-connection*. The *re-connection* phase primarily requires church leadership to use imagination in the contextualization of the gospel.

Churches in the *re-connection* phase need to engage their imaginations with the creativity of others who are successfully doing missional-incarnational ministry. This is a phase of *experimentation;* the church "visits Burning Man" before permanently changing its ministry mailing address to Black Rock City! Leadership concerns are:

Missional Leadership Must Discover

- What is our (church leadership's) vision for cultural transformation?
- What are some of the signs of exile in our community?
- How do we contextualize the gospel in our host community and what would our church look like?
- What are ways we can address the changes taking place in our community and our world?
- What are specific needs in our community? How can we meet these needs in ways that are incarnational in character?
- What kind of initial missional experiments for our church will likely morph into full-time missional ministry?

Among valuable resources for church leadership to consult in this phase are:

Resources for Phase 2

- The *Christianity Today* web-site: www.christianvisionproject.com. This link features "Faith and Culture." Among the invaluable resources on this site, church leadership ought to purchase: "Intersect Culture: Taking Your Group To A Place Where Faith & Culture Meet." This 6 session DVD features missional leaders (e.g., Andy Crouch, Frederica Mathewes-Green and Tim Keller) and helps leadership see people's needs in new ways for the purpose of creating a vision for cultural transformation.
- Your local community's website: read your community's vision with your eyes open to see the signs and your ears open to hear what the Spirit would say to you about the deepest longings of your community. Be creative in the ways you might contextualize the gospel in your community and imagine how you can be for your community what it cannot be for itself.
- Recall from Chapter 4, Martin Robertson's and Dwight Smith's insight: "Many churches in nations that are seeing a dramatic expansion of the kingdom are taking the natural and spontaneous passion of people and helping them to be much more intentional in their encounter with secular people."[14] Engage people in Interest Groups—groups formed around the natural and spontaneous passions of people in your church—with particular emphasis on prison ministry, AIDS/HIV and hospice care, among other social needs

in the community (social agencies in your community will welcome your help, but they need your follow-through!).
- Take your leadership on a "cross-cultural" adventure and work alongside of ministers in Chicago, Philadelphia, New York, Los Angeles, etc., for a couple of weeks and experience how messy ministry is supposed to be! (You might even show up in Black Rock City the end of August and the beginning of September!).
- Give those engaged in ministry to the social needs of the community space in the Sunday morning service to highlight what they are doing and how well received they are in the community (use media in creative/imaginative ways to feature congregational members engaged in missional ministry).
- Seek the opportunity to attend a John Perkins, Leonard Sweet, Dan Kimball, etc. type conference with your leadership. Brainstorm the many creative ways your church can manifest the presence of the kingdom of God in your community.[15]

Phase 3 begins with the changing of your permanent ministry address to "Black Rock City" and perhaps murmuring among your ecclesiastical neighbors and former parishioners about how you have become "like them"—sinners, the IRS or worse, the political left! You appear to be "a glutton and a drunkard" in the eyes of those entrenched in the center, but stay strong, you are not the first to be slandered because of incarnating divine compassion!

A MISSIONAL JOURNEY: PHASE 3: *RE-CREATE*: MINIMUM TIME: AN ORGANIC CHURCH IS ALWAYS ADAPTING—UNTIL THE RETURN OF JESUS CHRIST!

In this phase, your church enters missional life; ministry is messy, ministry is concentrated on the cultural margins, and ministry is culturally transforming—phrase 3 is the launching of "Vital Christianity" into your community! Your church no longer exists for itself; it is for the world what it cannot be for itself! Phase 3 is the practical application of a *politics of re-creation*.

In this phase leadership concerns are:

Missional Leadership Must Discover

- What is Jesus doing and where is he doing it in our community?
- How can we join Jesus where he is and give our lives away to others?

- How can we manifest the present kingdom of God through a politics of *re-form*, *re-connection* and *re-creation*?
- Who shares our passion for cultural transformation?
- Who can we partner with for the purpose of achieving our ministry goals?
- What are the "hurting places" in our city? Who (individuals or families) within our church is willing to relocate to these areas and help those on the margins connect with the resources of the community, reconcile them to the church, teach them new skills and help them find employment?
- Do we need co-ops, proximity spaces, youth centers, assisted living centers, etc.? How can we creatively finance these projects?
- Are there unique ethnic pockets and/or particular cultural interests (art, music, theatre, etc.) we can reach through proximity spaces?
- Are we working with children's advocacy organizations, juvenile detention centers, foster care and crisis pregnancy centers on a full-time basis?
- Do we need to open an international center to assist students with cultural change, personal needs and perhaps, English language skills from foreign nations who attend our local university and/or college?
- How can we house the homeless, feed the hungry and clothe the naked?

The compassion of a truly Vital Christianity, expressed through the missional church, is easily confused with Jesus' compassion; it invokes images in the minds of men and women redefining their view of the church, like Ryan from my Burning Man story: "Yeah, [Jesus' church] spends a lot time with tax collectors, prostitutes and sinners; just like all of us." Or perhaps the columnist for the Oregon State newspaper, the *Barometer*, would "change his mind" after seeing "Jesus sippin' a cappuccino at the Java Stop"!

The church's vocation is to follow Jesus to Burning Man and join with him there in ministry! Depending on your church's vision for cultural transformation, among valuable resources to consult in Phase 3 are:

Resources for Phase 3

- LA Dream Center: http;//www.dreamcenter.org
- Imago-Dei Church, Portland OR: http;//www.imagodeicommunity.org
- The Mosaic Church: http;//www.mosaic.org
- John M. Perkins Foundation for Reconciliation and Development: http;//www.jmpf.org
- Nishimura & Associates (Assists in the planning/development of Assisted Living Centers, Memory Care Facilities, Church construction, etc.): http://nishimuraassociates.com

A *politics of re-creation* calls the church to surrender her efforts to build or advance the Kingdom and rather engage in the implementation of the work already accomplished by Christ through the empowering presence of the Holy Spirit in church life and ministry.

Churches in the *re-create* phase not only see that the "world is changing," through their enactment of the gospel they are enabling the world around them to "see Jesus in the water"; to "feel him in the earth" and "smell him in the air" by being the presence of Christ in every corner of their "*cursed postmodern world.*"

CHURCH PLANTING

A brief statement about church planting is both timely and in order. A new church plant is open to new ideas; and it is open to experimentation and failure when it comes to the application of new ideas—church plants are willing to take risks!

New church plants are often evangelistic, creative and unstable—the instability is not only accepted as a part of their newness, but it also promotes ministry as messy instead of as the fruit of some strategic plan. Church plants therefore often encourage older churches to re-examine their ministry methods and seek new, innovative ways of penetrating the host community with the gospel.

Nevertheless, although a new church plant can initially appear very attractive, some believers eventually begin to seek out the stability, maturity and many opportunities for personal growth characteristic of older, established churches.[16]

Whether you are preparing to replant an existing church through the three phases: *re-form, re-connect* and *re-create*, or you are envisioning a new church plant, Tim Keller and the Redeemer Presbyterian's website provides in-depth biblical insight into church planting/replanting: http://www.redeemer.com/about_us/church_planting.

Also see, the Assemblies of God homepage, re: Church Planting: http://ag.org/top/. (The Assemblies of God has many sites featuring church planting in a variety of districts throughout the United States and the world). Both of these recommendations are typical of many, if not most, communions and the opportunities they offer for church planting.

NOTES

1. David Rapoza, *The Daily Barometer*, September 29, 2001, A4–5.
2. Ellen Haroutunian, "Postmodern Ministry: In Search of a Living Orthodoxy" http://www.anewkindofchristian.com, (12–22–07).
3. Jacques Derrida, *Of Grammatology*, trans. Gayatri Chakravorty Spivak (Baltimore, MD: The Johns Hopkins University Press, 1976), 158.

4. Jean-Francois Lyotard, *The Postmodern Condition: A Report on Knowledge* (Minneapolis, MN: University of Minnesota Press, 1984), xxiv, succinctly defines Post-Modernity as: "incredulity towards metanarratives." I realize the "hermeneutic of suspicion" is a self-defeating notion; it is itself, a truth-claim. However, the church ought not use apologetics in a manner that serves to only further alienate the culture.

5. Lyotard, The Postmodern Condition, 9.

6. Ludwig Wittgenstein, *Philosophical Investigations,* trans. G.E.M. Anscombe (New York: Macmillan Press, 1953), sec. 23.

7. Lyotard, The Postmodern Condition, 10.

8. Ibid.

9. Ibid., 20.

10. *Bonanza* and its linear storyline is replaced by *Lost* and its stacked narratives. Preaching in narrative by pastors, instead of linear power point presentations, resonates with congregations and the postmodern culture. Narrative is the most practical means by which to communicate truth in the postmodern context. Pastors can visit the website of Redeemer Presbyterian Church, Pastor Tim Keller, http://www.redeemer.com and Leonard Sweet, http://www.leonardsweet.com, for examples of narrative preaching.

11. Leonard Sweet, *The Gospel According to Starbucks* (Colorado Springs: WaterBrook Press, 2007), xi.

12. Lyotard, The Postmodern Condition, 23.

13. An excellent book to read during this phase is: Alan J. Roxburgh and Fred Romanuk, *The Missional Leader* (San Francisco, CA: Jossey-Bass, 2006).

14. Martin Robinson and Dwight Smith, *Invading Secular Space* (Oxford, UK: Monarch, 2003), 187.

15. An excellent book to read during this phase is: *The Church in Emerging Culture, Five Perspectives,* General Editor: Leonard Sweet (Grand Rapids, MI: Zondervan Publishers, 2003).

16. Timothy Keller, "Why Plant Churches," Redeemer City to City: http://redeemercitytocity.com/library.jsp?Library_item_param=19. Downloaded: 08/28/10.

Appendix One

Discipleship: Interactive Everything!

Remember Steve Bartman? Chicago Cubs fans will not soon forget him! Bartman was sitting in aisle 4, row 8, seat, 113 in Wrigley Field's left-field corner just beyond the foul line when he interfered with Moises Alou's effort to catch a foul ball in the 2003 National League Playoffs. Instead of the inning ending, the Marlins eventually scored and Florida defeated Chicago.

Steve Bartman, his Cubs hat pulled down to cover his eyes, his walkman still in place but instead of hearing play by play, it served to block out some of the threats coming from angry Cubs fans; his scarf pulled around his face to keep it from view of those who want to drag him out of the stadium and lynch him, is escorted under tight security out of the park. And the Cubs are denied yet again a trip to the World Series.

Cubs' fans tell me that on game day, Wrigley is the happiest place on earth. When the Cubs are in town, it's all about the experience; everyone participates together in loud, off-key singing and the telling of stories, especially legendary stories about the Cubs; and the beer and the hot dog consumption is awe-striking—nine innings of robust tailgate partying inside the stadium instead of the parking lot. Win or lose, Cubs fans are bound together in their love for the team on the North-Side.

But on the eve of October 14, 2003, Wrigley turned dark. The morning after, message boards read: "Death to Steve Bartman." Blogs urged fans to "seek revenge." T-Shirts were printed: "Sit down Steve;" "The Curse Lives—Thanks Steve." Doctored photos implicated Bartman in the destruction of the World Trade Center Towers. And another photo was a mug shot of Bartman as the primary suspect in the Washington D.C sniper shootings. Steve Bartman's infamy is unparalleled in modern sports history in the "Windy City"—Bartman is banned from Wrigley![1]

But Steve Bartman is a Chicago icon; he's what a true Cubs fan is all about. As a high fly ball off the bat of a Florida Marlin begins to pass out of the field of play, gradually curving towards aisle 4, row 8, seat 113, Bartman is ready. His eyes are fixed on the ball; he waits for it to reach the highest point of its arch and then begin to fall from the night sky over Wrigley. It's coming in his direction! He stretches out his left hand towards left-field and carefully watches the ball go into his open glove; he's got it! This isn't about getting a souvenir. Steve's not a passive spectator; he's participating in the action, he's there to ensure victory for the Cubs. And any Cubs' fan that believes he would not have done the same thing is probably not a true Cubs' fan.

Bartman should be the poster boy for Cubs baseball—he embodies the thrill of the experience and the joy of participating as the "tenth man" for one of America's most beloved teams. The long-suffering Cubs community has stood by their team and one another through the most difficult times. And no franchise in all of sport knows difficult times like the team on the North-Side.

But Cubs fans, from the governor to the ticket takers, fail to read the signs and consequently, they can't see how marketable the Bartman image really is in postmodern America—the Bartman image is *interactive everything*! Bartman is not only a symbol of what Cubs baseball is all about; his image is what discipleship is all about in the postmodern cultural context!

DISCIPLESHIP—INTERACTIVE EVERYTHING

Church leadership needs to create interactive environments for Christians to participate in the facilitation of their own discipleship. I propose (at least) four interactive environments for discipleship to take place: (1) Developing a Biblical World-View; (2) Practicing the Presence of Christ in the Market Place; (3) Participation in Cultural Transformation and (4) Participation in the Great Commission.

CULTIVATE A BIBLICAL WORLD-VIEW

Gordon Fee observes: "Probably the one feature that distances the New Testament church the most from its contemporary counterpart is its thoroughly eschatological perspective of all of life. In contrast to most of us, eschatology—a unique understanding of the time of the End—conditioned the early believers' existence in every way."[2]

N.T. Wright shares the story of Aleksandr Solzhenitsyn's return to Russia after twenty years of exile. During his journey, Solzhenitsyn greeted his fellow citizens in every town. However, he also greeted former Communist officials who themselves had tyrannized many of Solzhenitsyn's fellow citizens. In response to objections from some of his fellow Russians to his kind gestures towards these officials, Solzhenitsyn protested saying, "the line between good and evil is never simply between 'us' and 'them.' The line between good and evil runs through each one of us."[3] For the church to reveal to the world a new humanity it must *Re-Form*—the church must abandon the notion that the line between good and evil is between "us" (the church) and "them" (the secular culture), and embrace a Biblical world-view set in an eschatological frame.[4]

N.T. Wright discusses the four basic questions from which all worldviews are constructed: (1) Who are we?—(2) Where are we?—(3) What is wrong?—and (4) What is the solution?[5] Following are a set of concise responses, each set in an eschatological frame, to the four world view questions; these brief responses are, however, contextually related to the theme of this book—cultural transformation, and therefore, they point to the church's vocation. (See Chapter 5, Phase 1 Resources: Colson and Pearcy, *How Now Shall We Live?* for a clear, outstanding and exhaustive response to the four world view questions).

Who are we? The Kingdom has come in Christ; the Kingdom is a present reality—the gift of the Spirit brings awareness to the life of the believer that the messianic age has been inaugurated through the coming of Jesus Christ. An *inaugural eschatology* informs our regenerated conscience we are included in the promised new covenant (Jer. 31:31/Eph. 1:13–14); and we are the first-fruits of new creation, a new humanity, and a new covenant community (2 Cor. 5:17; Rev. 21:3–5a).

Where are we? A *realized eschatology* places the believer in a paradoxical context: the kingdom of God now present is the first-fruits of a still future kingdom. The Christian lives in an *already/not yet* tension—already, "the powers have been defeated"; Christ has reclaimed his creation—but not yet, are we freed from trials, suffering and the need to persevere in faith. The church is an eschatological community, "stamped with eternity" and therefore, God has brought the future into the present—personal regeneration in the present, is assurance that God will renew the whole of his creation.

What is the Problem? The human race is fallen—Genesis 3 is historical, not metaphorical; humanity is in an *actual* sin condition. Scripture describes the sinful condition of human nature—the corruption of our moral and spiritual nature—in Romans 1:18–3:20. And therefore, although God's wrath against the unrepentant is continually increasing towards "the day of wrath" when God's "righteous judgment will be revealed" (Rom. 2:5), men love darkness "instead of light" because our deeds are evil (John 3:19).

"It may fairly be claimed," writes J.I. Packer, "that the Fall narrative gives the only convincing explanation of the perversity of human nature that the world has ever seen. Pascal said that the doctrine of original sin seems an offense to reason, but once accepted it makes total sense of the entire human condition. He was right, and the same thing may and should be said of the Fall narrative itself."[6]

What is the Solution? In Christ, God has graciously revealed his *restoration eschatology*—humanity is no longer in exile, our sins are forgiven and God has both renewed the covenant with Israel and extended its full thrust to the Gentile world! The church's recovery of its vocation results in its participation with the eschatological Spirit in making all things new. The church is to both enact and proclaim the gospel throughout all the earth; the Spirit enables the church to follow through in obedience to God's calling.

WORLD-VIEWS AND SEMIOTICS

N.T. Wright observes: "the stories that express the worldview, and the answers which it provides to the questions of identity, environment, evil and eschatology, are expressed ... in cultural *symbols*.[7] The Son of Man's proclamation—"The kingdom of God is near. Repent and believe the good news!"—was consistently followed by two outstanding signs or symbols: the delivering of those tormented by demonic spirits and the healing of the infirmed (e.g., Mark 1:15; 21–27; 29–34). These two signs pointed to Israel's deliverance from exile and their restoration to the covenant. These two signs point to our culture's deliverance from exile and restoration to the covenant—Jesus has restored the full thrust of the covenant to "all nations."

Eschatology is the essential framework of the New Testament, and consequently, the recovery of a Biblical world-view enables the believer to see the world through a symbolic paradigm framed in an inaugural, realized and restoration eschatology; and tragically, also the fall of the human race.

PRACTICING THE PRESENCE OF
CHRIST IN THE MARKET PLACE

Gordon Fee emphatically remarks: ". . .I am convinced that the only worthwhile theology is that which is translated into life."[8] How can a theology of the Spirit, that is to say: "the newly constituted eschatological people of God are Spirit people;" they live by the life-giving Spirit (Gal. 5:25; 2 Cor. 3:3; 6) and "they walk by the Spirit and they are led by the Spirit"[9]—be translated into the everyday life of the believer in a way that will change the lives of those around them in the market-place?

A complete answer to this question requires another book and therefore, my response is merely intended to be a signpost to the interactive environment needed for Christians to discover imaginative and creative ways of practicing the presence of Christ in the market place.[10]

For the believer to effectively practice the presence of Christ in the marketplace she must first learn to think theologically—an interactive setting for the purpose of discovering creative ways of understanding the foundations of the Christian faith: the authority of the Bible, the Trinity, the Incarnation, Salvation (Soteriology), the Holy Spirit (Pneumatology), and Eschatology is required.[11] The Holy Spirit, his personhood, and eschatological purposes should be a separate and thorough discussion.[12] Practicing the presence of Christ in the marketplace requires an awareness of how the Spirit empowers the believer's life.

Practicing the presence of Christ in the market place requires Christians to discern "signs of exile" (e.g., indications of separation and/or estrangement in the lives of those around them), and humbly act in ways that the person in need is incapable of doing for themselves.

How can believers be for un-regenerated people (non-Christians) what they cannot be for themselves? The "natural man" (the non-Christian) is incapable of returning from exile in their own power (their personal sense of separation or estrangement); they are incapable of the forgiveness of their sins (and dealing with their personal guilt) and they are incapable of coming into covenant relationship with the living God (and all of the grand implications for the individual and a nation involved with God's presence in the life of a human being and culture)[13]—they need the life and message of the believer!

Jesus said, "So in everything, do to others what you would have them do to you, for this sums up the Law and the Prophets" (Matthew 7:12). The reader will recall (chapter 3) how the "Golden Rule" inspired William Wilberforce's political philosophy.

The four pillars of Wilberforce's political philosophy are: (1) conscientious stewardship; (2) respect for the rights of others; (3) advancing the views of others and (4) the promotion of the happiness of others.

Regarding stewardship, Wilberforce stressed each individual is endowed by God with "means and occasions . . . of improving ourselves, or of promoting the happiness of others."[14] The conscientious stewardship of God's blessings upon individuals is to be used for the common good. This is a sacred duty, especially for Christians. Christians ought to "set the bar" for professionalism, performance and productivity in the work-place—the Christian ought to be the example of what an employer (or client) desires in an employee (or proprietor).

The grounds for every philanthropic and human rights issue is the Golden Rule in Wilberforce's political philosophy. The second political pillar, respect for the rights of others, requires "every one to regulate his conduct by the golden rule of doing to others as in similar circumstances we would have them do to us; and the path of duty will be clear before him...."[15] The Christian may not always, perhaps rarely, be reciprocated for their kindness, but the believer must persevere in honoring other people and meeting their needs, before they take care of their own needs. The Christian perseveres not for the sake of reward, but in obedience to the Scripture that calls us to do all things as unto Christ (Col. 3:17). And if the believer is faithful, God will light their path before them.

Promoting the views of others, the third of Wilberforce's political ideals, involves the practical application of the Golden Rule: place the views of others before the self—hear with understanding what is in the hearts of other people. The Christian does not promote falsehood over truth, immorality over morality or unrighteousness over righteousness but rather, she patiently and respectfully opens her heart to the views, philosophies or reflections of other people out of respect for them. The unbeliever is much more likely to hear a presentation of the Gospel from a believer who themselves have patiently and respectfully listened to their heart than from a believer who was impatient and intolerant towards them.

Wilberforce's fourth political strategy is the promotion of the happiness of others. Whereas Jefferson's ideal was the personal "pursuit of happiness," Wilberforce believed it was better to promote the happiness of others; indeed this would serve to promote one's own happiness in fuller, more meaningful ways. The Christian ought to pray for a conscience sensitive to the needs of others, and understanding of how to appropriately care for them.

If the Christian is committed to discovering ways and means of relating to the deepest longings of people who work with them in the market place, they will be, for others, the presence of Christ. The selflessness and compassion of the believer—"the abiding eloquence of a Christian life"—in the market place will significantly contribute to the harmony of relationships among people, changed lives and ultimately, God's glory.

Believers committed to practicing the presence of Christ in the market place need an interactive environment in which to meet and share experiences, encourage one another, and pray for one another.

PARTICIPATION IN CULTURAL TRANSFORMATION

Whereas the subject matter of this book is cultural transformation, for the purpose of discipleship, church leadership should consult chapter 5, "Jesus at the Java Stop" and develop creative and imaginative ways for all age groups in the church to participate in cultural transformation. How can children be the presence of Christ in their school? What are some ways children can participate in cultural transformation? Church leadership should seek practical ways for all age groups to effectively apply kingdom politics to their particular demographic.

PARTICIPATION IN THE GREAT COMMISSION

Easter calls the Church to go and make disciples of all nations; Pentecost clothes the church in power for the sake of achieving Easter's calling. The work of the Spirit in the life of the believer calls them to not merely hear about the Great Commission, but to experience it! Believers are called to participate in the Great Commission locally and "to the ends of the earth" through church organized missions trips. Believers are called to expose their lives to the rich images of Christian heritage, tradition and missions firsthand; they are called to commitment to loving, life-changing relationships in every corner of the earth.

The compassion of Jesus Christ breaks the heart of the believer, particularly in poverty-stricken contexts in third-world nations. The future of the church is in Latin America, Asia and Africa—believers who experience the power of Christ's Spirit in these missions-contexts return ready to transform the culture in which they live.

CONCLUSION: 21ST CENTURY DISCIPLESHIP IS INTERACTIVE EVERYTHING

These four interactive environments for discipleship are hardly exhaustive, nevertheless, in principle and practice, discipleship in the postmodern and post-postmodern context is *inter-active everything!* Effective discipleship is E-P-I-C: Christians need first-hand **E**xperiences; Christians need to **P**articipate in and facilitate one another's discipleship; Christian discipleship **I**nteracts with symbols, images and traditions in a *re-forming, re-connecting,* and *re-creating* Spirit-empowered **C**ommunity.

NOTES

1. My primary source for this introduction is: Wayne Drehe, "Foul Play, On the Trail of the Most Reclusive Man in Sports," http://sports.espn.go.com/espn/eticket/story?page=bartman, 1–11–2008.

2. Gordon Fee, *God's Empowering Presence* (Peabody, MA: Hendrickson Publishers, 1994), 803.

3. N.T. Wright, *Evil and the Justice of God* (Downers Grove, Ill.: Inter-Varsity Press, 2006), 38.

4. The Barna Group, "Barna Survey Examines Changes in Worldview Among Christians over the Past 13 Years," March 6, 2009, reports that less than 1 in 5, 19%, of born-again Christians think in terms of a biblical world-view. Christians, clergy and lay-persons' mindset, is largely shaped by modernity; modernism is the source of the radical dualism characteristic of many contemporary Christians.

5. N.T. Wright, *The New Testament and the People of God* (Minneapolis, MN: Fortress Press, 1992), 132–33. *The New Testament and the People of God* is an excellent text for church leadership to reference for the full development of a Christian World-View Also, see Wright's *Jesus and the Victory of God,* 443–51.

6. J.I. Packer, *Concise Theology* (Wheaton, Ill.: Tyndale House Publishers, 1993), 81.

7. Ibid.

8. Gordon Fee, God's Empowering Presence, 3.

9. Ibid., 855.

10. Books that give a complete answer include: N.T. Wright, *Simply Christian, Why Christianity Makes Sense* (San Francisco: Harper, 2006) and Leonard Sweet, *Soul Tsunami* (Grand Rapids, MI.: Zondervan, 1999).

11. I recommend church leadership consult two extraordinary books: Timothy Keller, *The Reason for God, Belief in an Age of Skepticism* (New York: Dutton, 2008); J.I. Packer, *Knowing God* (Downers Grove, Ill.: Inter-Varsity Press, 1973).

12. I recommend Gordon Fee's voluminous work for reference purposes: *God's Empowering Presence* (Peabody, MA.: Hendrickson Publishers, 1994) and J.I. Packer, *Keep In Step With The Spirit* (Tarrytown, N.Y.: Fleming H. Revell Co. 1984) and Roger Stronstad, *Spirit, Scripture & Theology, A Pentecostal Perspective* (Baguio City, Philippines, Asia Pacific Theological Seminary Press, 1995).

13. Educational systems, hospitals, orphanages, care for the poor, the homeless, widows, the dying, the mentally handicapped, and visiting the imprisoned have their origins in the gospel.

14. Belmonte, William Wilberforce, 177.

15. Ibid.

Appendix Two

Web Sites

http://www.allelon.net/missional_resources/church_survey.cfm
http://www.anewkindofconversation.com (Myron Penner, Brian McLaren and others address Postmodern Culture)
http://www.burningman.com (Burning Man, Black Rock City, NV)
http://www.christianvisionproject.com (*Christianity Today*, Faith and Culture)
http://www.ci.corvallis.or.us (Corvallis, OR)
http://www.dreamcenter.org (LA Dream-center)
http://www.etsjets.org (Evangelical Theological Society)
http://www.imagodeicommunity.org (Imago-Dei Church, Portland, OR)
http://www.iwsfla.org (Robert E. Webber Institute for Worship Studies)
http://www.jmpf.org (John M. Perkins Foundation for Reconciliation and Development)
http://www.leonardsweet.com (Leonard Sweet)
http://www.lionofjudah.tribulationforces.com (Apologetics and Postmodernism)
http://www.mosaic.org (The Mosaic Church, LA)
http://www.nextreformation.com (Ekklesia, Transition, Leadership and Formation)
http://www.ntwrightpage.com (N. T. Wright home-page)
http://www.preachingplus.com (Leonard Sweet)
http://www.redeemer.com (Redeemer Presbyterian, NYC)
http://www.refuseoftheworld.org (The Refuse Church, Colorado Springs, CO)
http://www.sanfrancisco.cityserach.com (re: Subterranean Shoe Store, San Francisco, CA)
http://www.scumoftheearth.org (The Scum of the Earth Church, Denver, CO)
http://www.spartacus-schoolnet.com.uk (William Wilberforce)
http://www.spu.edu (Seattle Pacific University, Seattle, WA)

http://www.stevekmccoy.com ("Reformissionary," Tim Keller, Redeemer Presbyterian, NYC)
http://www.thebolgblog.typepad.com (Ryan Bolger Blog, Emergent Church Leader)
http://www.tcpc.org (Center for Progressive Christianity)
http://www.the-park.net (Clapham Connection, UK)
http://www.wilberforce.org (Charles Colson – Wilberforce Forum)
http://www.xenos.org (Apologetics in the postmodern culture)
http://www.yale.edu (Yale Center for Faith and Culture)

Bibliography

Adler, Jerry. "In Search of the Spiritual." *Newsweek.* September 5, 2005, 46–52.
Alcock, Richard A. *World Literature.* New York: Greystone, 1957.
Anderson, J.N.D. *Christianity: The Witness of History.* Downers Grove, IL: InterVarsity Press, 1970.
Ashford, Bruce R. "Wittgenstein's Theologians? A Survey of Ludwig Wittgenstein's Impact on Theology." *Journal of the Evangelical Theological Society* 50, no. 2, (June 2007): 367–375.
Archer, Gleason. *An Encyclopedia of Bible Difficulties.* Minneapolis, MN: Bethany Fellowship, 1982.
Augustine of Hippo. *The City of God.* Vol. 2 of *Basic Writings of Saint Augustine.* Edited by Whitney J. Oates. 1948. Reprint, Grand Rapids, MI: Baker, 1992.
Bauer, Walter. *A Greek-English Lexicon of the New Testament and Other Early Christian Literature.* Chicago: The University of Chicago, 1979.
Beckwith, Francis. *Baha'i.* Minneapolis, MN: Bethany Fellowship, 1985.
Belmonte, Kevin. *William Wilberforce, A Hero for Humanity.* Grand Rapids, MI: Zondervan, 2007.
Blomberg, Craig L. *Contagious Holiness: Jesus' Meals With Sinners.* Downers Grove, IL: InterVarsity, 2005.
———. *Interpreting The Parables.* Downers Grove, IL: InterVarsity, 1990.
Bono. "The 54th Annual National Prayer Breakfast Speech, February 2, 2006." *The Worshipper,* Summer, 2006.
Bolger, Ryan. "A Brief Snapshot of the Emerging Church." The BlogBlog: Transient Thoughts on Following Jesus in Postmodern Cultures, entry posted September 16, 2005, http://thebolgblog.typepad.com/thebolgblog/2005/09/index.html (accessed February 7, 2008).
———. "Does the World Know Jesus Better Than The Church Does?" The BlogBlog: Transient Thoughts on Following Jesus in Postmodern Cultures, entry posted September 16, 2005, http://thebolgblog.typepad.com/thebolgblog/2005/09/index.html (accessed February 7, 2008).

Brown, Colin, ed. *The New International Dictionary of New Testament Theology.* Vol. I. Grand Rapids, MI: Zondervan Publishing House, 1975.

Bruce, F.F.. *The New Testament Documents: Are They Reliable?* Downers Grove, IL: Inter-Varsity Press, 1977.

Borg, Marcus, J. *Conflict, Holiness, and Politics in the Teaching of Jesus.* New York: Mellen, 1984.

Byassee, Jason. "Emerging Model: A Visit to Jacob's Well." *The Christian Century,* September 2006.

Card, Michael. *Immanuel, Reflections on the Life of Christ.* Nashville, TN: Thomas Nelson, 1990.

Carnes, Tony. "New York's New Hope." *Christianity Today,* December 2004.

Casey, P. M. *The Son of Man.* London: SPCK, 1979.

Cole, Neil. *Organic Church.* San Francisco: Jossey-Bass, 2005.

Colson, Charles, and Nancy Pearcey, *How Now Shall We Live?* Wheaton, IL: Tyndale Publishers, 1999.

———. *Loving God.* Grand Rapids, MI: Zondervan Publishers, 1983.

Dahle, Lars. "Acts 17 As an Apologetic Model" *Whitefield Briefing* 7, no. 1, March 2002. Reprint, *Culture Watch,* http://www.damaris.org/content/content.php?type=5&id=220 (accessed December 22, 2007.

Derrida, Jacques. *Deconstruction in a Nutshell.* Edited by John D. Caputo. New York: Fordham University, 1997.

———. *Of Grammatology.* Translated by Gayatri Chakravorty Spivak. Baltimore, MD: The Johns Hopkins University, 1976.

———. *Writing and Difference.* Translated by Alan Bass. Chicago: University of Chicago, 1978.

Eagleton, Terry. "Awakening from Modernity." *Times Literary Supplement,* 20, February 1987.

———. *Literary Theory.* Minneapolis: University of Minnesota, 1983.

Ellis, E. Earle. *The Gospel of Luke.* London: Nelson, 1966.

Fee, Gordon D. *God's Empowering Presence.* Peabody, MA.: Hendrickson Publishers, 1994.

———. *The First Epistle to the Corinthians.* Grand Rapids, MI: William B. Eerdmans, 1987.

Frost, Michael, and Hirsch, Alan. *The Shape of Things to Come.* Peabody, MA: Hendrickson, 2003.

Furneaux, Robin. *William Wilberforce.* London: Hamish Hamilton, 1974.

Geisler, Norman. *Christian Apologetics.* Grand Rapids, MI: Baker Book House, 1976.

Green, J. B. *The Gospel of Luke.* Grand Rapids, MI: William B. Eerdmans, 1997.

Greenleaf, Simon. *The Testimony of the Evangelists Examined by the Rules of Evidence Administered in Courts of Justice.* 1874. Reprint, Grand Rapids, MI: Baker, 1984.

Grenz, Stanley. *A Primer on Postmodernism.* Grand Rapids, MI: William B. Eerdmans, Publishing Co., 1996.

———, and John Franke, *Beyond Foundationalism: Shaping Theology in a Postmodern Context.* Louisville, KY: Westminister/Knox, 2001.
Groothuis, Douglas. "Why Truth Matters Most: An Apologetic for Truth-Seeking in Postmodern Times." *Journal of the Evangelical Theological Society* 47, no. 3 (September 2004): 441.
Habermas, Gary R., and Michael R. Licona. *The Case for the Resurrection of Jesus.* Grand Rapids, MI: Kregel Publications, 2004.
Halvey, Elie. *A History of the English People in the 19th Century,* Vol. 1 of *England in 1815.* London: Ernest Benn, 1949.
Hancock, Christopher D. "The Shrimp Who Stopped Slavery: Wilberforce versus Slavery." *Christian History* 53, (Winter 1997).
Hansen, Collin, "How Then Shall We Politick?" *Christianity Today,* August 2006. http://www.christianitytoday.com/ct/2006/august/9.38.html (accessed February 7, 2008).
Haroutunian, Ellen, "Postmodern Ministry: In Search of a Living Orthodoxy" http://www.anewkindofchristian.com (accessed December 22, 2007).
Hengel, Martin. *Studies in Early Christology.* Edinburgh: T. and T. Clark, 1995.
Hilario, Conrad. "No Need For Apologetics? Postmodernism's Affect On Christian Apologetics." http://www.xenos.org/essays/NoNeedForApologetics.html (accessed December 22, 2007).
Hill, Clifford. *The Wilberforce Connection.* Oxford, UK: Monarch Books, 2004.
Hjarmalson, Len. "Post-Modern Possibilities" http://nextreformation.com/wp-admin/articles/postmod1g.htm (accessed October 14, 2005).
Hooker, M. D. *The Son of Man in Mark.* London: SPCK, 1967.
Horton, Michael S. *"How The Kingdom Comes."* Christianity Today, January 2006.
Howse, Ernest Marshall. *Saints in Politics: The Clapham Sect and the Growth of Freedom.* London: Allen and Unwin, 1952.
Friedrich, Gerhard, and Gerard Kittel, eds. *Theological Dictionary of the New Testament,* Vols. I, III-IX (Grand Rapids, MI: William B. Eerdmans, 1976)
Josephus. "Antiquities of the Jews." In *Josephus: Complete Works,* translated by William Whiston. Grand Rapids, MI: Kregel, 1960
Keener, Craig S. *Matthew.* Downers Grove, IL: InterVarsity, 1997.
Kenyon, Sir Fredric G. *The Bible and Archaeology.* New York: Harper, 1940.
Killen, Connell, and Mark Silk. eds. *Religion and Public Life in the Pacific Northwest.* Toronto, ON: Roman and Littlefield, 2004.
Kimball, Dan. *The Emerging Church.* Grand Rapids, MI: Zondervan, 2003.
King Jr., Martin Luther. *Strength to Love.* New York: Harper and Row, 1963.
Klausner, Joseph. *Jesus of Nazareth.* New York: Macmillan, 1925.
Land, Richard. *The Divided States of America?* Nashville, TN: Thomas Nelson, 2007.
Lane, William. *The Gospel According to Mark.* Grand Rapids, MI: William B. Eerdmans, 1974.
Larkin Jr., William J. "The Recovery of Luke-Acts as 'Grand Narrative' for the Church's Evangelistic and Edification Tasks in a Postmodern Age." *Journal of the Evangelical Theological Society* 43, 3 (September 2000): 405–416.

Leffel, Jim. "Engineering Life, Human Rights in a Postmodern Age." *Christian Research Journal* 20, no. 1 (September-October, 1997).

———. "Understanding Today's Postmodern University," http://www.xenos.org/essays/pomouniv.htm (accessed December 22, 2007).

Lewis, Allan. *Between Cross and Resurrection: A Theology of Holy Saturday*. Grand Rapids, MI: William B. Eerdmans, 2001.

Lindars, B. *Jesus Son of Man*. London: SPCK, 1983.

Lynch, Gordon. *Understanding Theology and Popular Culture*. Malden, MA: Blackwell, 2005.

Lyotard, Jean-Francois. *The Postmodern Condition: A Report on Knowledge*. Minneapolis: University of Minnesota, 1984.

———. *The Postmodern Explained*. Minneapolis: University of Minnesota, 1993.

Marshall, I. Howard. *The Gospel of Luke: A Commentary on the Greek Text*. Exeter, UK: Paternoster, 1978.

———. *The Origins of New Testament Christology*. Updated ed. Downers Grove, IL: InterVarsity, 1990.

Matzat, Don. "Apologetics in a Postmodern Age." *Issues, Etc., Journal* 2, no. 5 (Fall 1997): 1–14.

McGrath, Alister E. *Bridge-Building: Effective Christian Apologetics*. Leicester, UK: InterVarsity, 1992.

———. "The Challenge of Pluralism for The Contemporary Christian Church." *Journal of the Evangelical Theological Society* 35, 3 (September 1992): 361–373.

———. "The Christian Church's Response to Pluralism." *Journal of the Evangelical Theological Society* 35, 4 (December 1992): 487–501.

McLaren, Brian. *Reinventing Your Church*. Grand Rapids, MI: Zondervan, 1998.

———. *The Church on the Other Side*. Grand Rapids, MI: Zondervan, 1998.

McRoberts, Kerry, *New Age or Old Lie?* Peabody, MA: Hendrickson Publishers, 1989.

Middleton, J. Richard, and Brian J. Walsh. *Truth Is Stranger Than It Used to Be: Biblical Faith in a Postmodern Age*. Downers Grove, IL: InterVarsity, 1995.

Milbank, J. "The End of Dialogue." In *Christian Uniqueness Reconsidered: The Myth of a Pluralistic Theology of Religions*, ed. G. D'Costa; Maryknoll, NY: Orbis, 1990, 174–91.

Moll, Rob. "The New Monasticism." *Christianity Today*, September 2005.

Montgomery, John W. *Human Rights and Human Dignity*. Grand Rapids, MI: Zondervan, 1986.

———. *The Law Above the Law*. Minneapolis: Bethany Fellowship, 1975.

Moreland, J. P. "Truth, Contemporary Philosophy, and the Postmodern Turn." *Journal of the Evangelical Theological Society* 48, no. 1, (March 2005): 77.

Nickelsburg, George W. E. "Son of Man." In *The Anchor Bible Dictionary,* Vol. 6. Edited by David Noel Freedman. New York: Doubleday, 1992.

Olthuis, James H. "A Cold and Comfortless Hermeneutic or a Warm and Trembling Hermeneutic: A Conversation with John D. Caputo." *Christian Scholar's Review,* 19, no. 4 (1990).

Packer, J.I. *Keep In Step With The Spirit.* Tarrytown, N.Y.: Fleming H. Revell Co., 1984.

Pannenberg, W. "Religious Pluralism and Conflicting Truth Claims." In *Christian Uniqueness Reconsidered: The Myth of a Pluralistic Theology of Religions.* ed. G. D'Costa; Maryknoll, NY: Obis, 1990.

Pattison, Bonnie L. *Poverty in the Theology of John Calvin.* Eugene, OR: Pickwick Publications, 2006.

Penner, Myron B. "Postmodern Apologetics?" *A New Kind of Conversation,* November 5, 2005. http://www.anewkindofconversation.com (accessed December 22, 2007).

Perkins, John. *Let Justice Roll Down.* New York: Regal, 1977.

———. ed. *Restoring At Risk Communities.* Grand Rapids, MI: Baker, 1995.

Phillips, Timothy R., and Dennis L. Okholm, eds. *Christian Apologetics in the Postmodern World.* Downers Grove, IL: InterVarsity, 1995.

Pollock, John. *Wilberforce.* London: Constable, 1977.

Pura, Andrew Murray. *Vital Christianity.* Toronto, ON: Clements, 2003.

Rapoza, David, "Got Faith," *The Daily Barometer.* September 29, 2001.

Robinson, Martin, and Dwight Smith. *Invading Secular Space.* Oxford, UK: Monarch, 2003.

Rosman, Doreen, M. *Evangelicals and Culture.* London: Croom Helm, 1984.

Roxburgh, Alan J. & Romanuk, Fred. *This Missional Leader.* Jossey-Bass: San Francisco, CA: 2006

Rowland, Christopher C. *The Open Heaven: A Study of Apocalyptic in Judaism and Early Christianity.* New York: Crossroad, 1982.

Sider, Ronald J. *The Scandal of the Evangelical Conscience: Why Are Christians Living Just Like the Rest of the World?* Grand Rapids, MI: Baker, 2005.

———, and Knippers, Diane, eds. *Toward an Evangelical Public Policy.* Grand Rapids, MI: Baker, 2005.

Stein, R. H. *Luke.* Nashville, TN: Broadman, 1992.

Storkey, Alan. *Jesus and Politics.* Grand Rapids, MI: Baker Academic, 2005.

Strauss, D.F. *Das Leben Jesu.* Darmstadt: Wissenschaftliche Buchgesellschaft, 1835.

Stronstad, Roger, *Spirit, Scripture & Theology: A Pentecostal Perspective.* Baguio City, Philippines: Asia Pacific Theological Seminary Press, 1995.

Sweet, Leonard, ed. *The Church in Emerging Culture.* Grand Rapids, MI: Zondervan, 2003.

———. *The Gospel According to Starbucks.* Colorado Springs: WaterBrook, 2007.

———. *The Three Hardest Words in the World to Get Right.* Colorado Springs: WaterBrook, 2006.

———. *Postmodern Pilgrims.* Nashville, TN: Broadman and Holmes, 2000.

———. *Soul Tsunami.* Grand Rapids, MI: Zondervan, 1999.

Toulmin, Stephen Edelston. *The Uses of Argument.* Cambridge, UK: Cambridge University, 1958.

Vaughan, David J. *Statesman and Saint: The Principled Politics of William Wilberforce.* Nashville, TN: Highland, 2002.

Wallis, Jim. *God's Politics*. San Francisco: Harper, 2005.
Westfall, Merold. *Suspicion and Faith*. Grand Rapids, MI: William B. Eerdmans, 1993.
Wilberforce, William. *A Practical View of Christianity*. Peabody, MA: Hendrickson, 1996.
Willard, Dallas. *The Divine Conspiracy*. San Francisco: Harper, 1997.
Witherington III, B. *The Christology of Jesus*. Minneapolis: Fortress, 1990.
——. *The Gospel of Mark: A Socio-Rhetorical Commentary*. Grand Rapids, MI: William B. Eerdmans, 2001.
Wittgenstein, Ludwig. *Tractatus Logico-Philosophicus*. London: Routledge, 1974.
——, *Philosophical Investigations*. trans. G.E.M. Anscombe. New York: Macmillan Press, 1953.
Wright, N. T. "A Conversation With N. T. Wright, The Gospel and Cultural Engagement," *Response* 28, no. 2 (Summer, 2005), 1–7.
——. "Christian Origins and the Resurrection of Jesus: The Resurrection of Jesus as a Historical Problem." *Sewanee Theological Review* 41, no. 2 (Easter1998), 1–13.
——. "Early Traditions and the Origins of Christianity." *Sewanee Theological Review* 41, no. 2 (Easter1998), 1–12.
——. *Jesus and the Victory of God*. Minneapolis: Fortress, 1996.
——. "One God, One Lord, One People: Incarnational Christology for a Church in a Pagan Environment." *Ex Auditu: Journal of the North Park Symposium on the Theological Interpretation of Scripture* 7 (January 2005), 1–13.
——. "The Bible and Christian Imagination." *Response* 28, no. 2, (May 2005), 1–6.
——. *The Challenge of Jesus: Rediscovering Who Jesus Was and Is*. Downers Grove, IL: InterVarsity, 1999.
——. "The Christian Challenge in the Postmodern World," *Response* 28, no. 2 (May 2005), 1–2.
——. *The New Testament and the People of God*. Minneapolis: Fortress, 1992.
——. *The Resurrection of the Son of God*. Minneapolis: Fortress, 2003.
——. "The Resurrection and the Postmodern Dilemma," *Sewanee Theological Review* 41, no. 2 (Easter 1998).
Zacharias, Ravi. "Reaching the Happy Thinking Pagan: How Can We Present the Christian Message to Postmodern People?" In *Growing Your Church through Evangelism and Outreach*. Library of Christian Leadership, edited by Marshall Shelley. New York: Random House, 1996.

www.ingramcontent.com/pod-product-compliance
Lightning Source LLC
Chambersburg PA
CBHW031554300426
44111CB00006BA/312